Kona to the rescue!

Kona kept vigil at the window, trembling as giant pines bent their icy heads to the ground and jumping at the sharp sounds of thick bark breaking.

"What are we going to do, Gwendolyn?" Kona asked, his big head casting a giant shadow over her bowl. "Stumpy is in serious trouble."

"Yes," Gwendolyn answered, nodding. "It's serious, very serious. Even if her tree is still standing, she will be trapped in her nest. And the ice...the babies..."

"I have to help her," Kona said, pacing in circles around the living room.

The old crab looked at the dog and spoke gently, "Her chance of surviving seems very unlikely."

Kona took a deep breath and, with eyes wide and sincere, answered, "Whether she is alive or not, Gwendolyn, I have to take care of her."

Cynthia Rylant

Gooseberry Park

WITH ILLUSTRATIONS BY
Arthur Howard

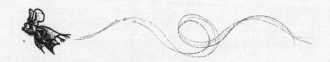

Harcourt, Inc.

Orlando   Austin   New York   San Diego   Toronto   London

Thank you, AJ and DP

For information about permission to reproduce selections from this book,
write to trade.permissions@hmhco.com or to Permissions, Houghton Mifflin Harcourt
Publishing Company, 3 Park Avenue, 19th Floor, New York, New York 10016

www.hmhco.com

First Harcourt paperback edition 2007

The Library of Congress has cataloged the hardcover edition as follows:
Rylant, Cynthia.
Gooseberry Park/Cynthia Rylant; illustrated by Arthur Howard—1st ed.
p.   cm.
Summary: When a storm separates Stumpy the squirrel
from her newborn babies, her animal friends come to the rescue.
[1. Squirrels—Fiction.   2. Animals—Fiction.]   I. Title.
PZ7.R982Go   1995
[Fic]—dc20   94-11578
ISBN 978-0-15-232242-7
ISBN 978-0-15-206159-3 pb

The text was set in Cheltenham Book.
Designed by Camilla Filancia
Printed in the United States of America
24 2021
4500830752

To Caitlyn Cushner and Kona

Contents

Contents

CHAPTER ONE

A New Nest

All new mothers have a nesting instinct, even human mothers who haven't any idea how to build a nest.

While human mothers are waiting for their babies to be born, their nesting instinct causes them to do the silliest things, such as taking all the pots out of one cabinet and all the pans out of another and switching them. Human mothers don't know why they are doing this except that some little voice in their heads is saying "Keep busy! Keep busy!"

A sensible *rabbit* mother who hears this little voice will simply pluck her fur with her teeth to make

A New Nest

a nice warm baby bed for the near future. But a mixed-up human mother will just wander about her kitchen, switching her cabinets for no reason at all.

Thus it was a good thing that Stumpy was a squirrel. She knew a nesting instinct when she felt one, and she knew what to do about it.

For many days now, every part of her red squirrel body had been shouting "Keep busy! Keep busy!" And was she ever keeping busy! For the new nest she was building, she had collected the choicest twigs and the finest leaves and—because she was

A New Nest

sure of what was about to happen—bits of the pink-dotted, blue-flowered, or green-starred material that could be had by a little digging in the can behind the town sewing shop. One morning she had even happened upon a bit of cloth decorated with pictures of little red squirrels carrying small, brown nut sacks, and she nearly fainted away. It was better than she could have hoped for her new babies.

And new babies indeed were what she was about to have. Babies to love, to keep clean, to bring up close against her fur in the dark night. Stumpy was about to become a mother and, oh, was she proud.

And busy. Quite busy.

Carefully she lined her new nest with the twigs, the leaves, and the bits of beautiful cloth. She had recently moved from an old locust tree on the south side of Gooseberry Park to a pin oak on the east. She had moved because, like most who live alone, Stumpy had been rather relaxed about her house-keeping, and her old nest had become difficult to move around in. You see, Stumpy was a collector, and her nest was full of treasures. She had tremendous energy, and after she had found as many acorns and pinecones as could be eaten by one little squirrel, she burned up the rest of her energy by collecting.

Stumpy collected these things:

> tabs from soda pop cans
> empty yogurt cups
> gum wrappers
> coins
> ice-cream sticks
> straws
> feathers
> pretty pebbles
> little balls lost by children
> nuts, bolts, screws, tacks
> twist ties
> rubber bands

Her most beautiful treasure of all, though, had been a lovely watch that glowed in the dark. Two winters ago, she had found it lying on top of a picnic table. She took it to her nest and didn't realize until

A New Nest

evening what a marvel it was. As darkness came, the watch began to shine and Stumpy's nest became bathed in a soft green light. Animals who passed at night were drawn to it. Everyone came to see it. And news spread far and wide of the glow-in-the-dark nest in Gooseberry Park.

A New Nest

Unfortunately, the news spread too far and too wide. Someone came one day and stole that watch from Stumpy's nest. Stumpy never found it again, though for weeks she sat high in her tree at night and looked out over the park, hoping to see that soft green glow.

She never did.

Still, Stumpy had other treasures. In fact, too many treasures, and her collection had gotten all out of control. Stumpy knew that no self-respecting mother of several young children could have her babies sleeping among wood screws and twist ties.

So she found a new tree and built a clean nest and organized her collection to give plenty of room for her babies. Her friend Kona would be proud of her housecleaning. Each time she collected something new, Kona would say to her:

"Stump, you've too many things."

And she would answer, "Not things. Treasure."

And Kona would say, "Stump, my owner Professor Albert has a chess set crafted in pure silver. A crystal punch bowl. And a set of Limoges china. *That's* treasure."

A New Nest

Well, what could a Labrador dog know about treasure anyway, thought Stumpy. Kona was a good friend, a fine friend. But he had no imagination. If he had, he'd be living in the park collecting feathers and balls instead of sitting in a boring ranch house with Professor Albert.

Stumpy had babies and copper pennies and even the chance of finding another glow-in-the-dark watch to look forward to. She went on carefully layering her maple leaves and flowered cloth and green twigs into a safe, warm pocket.

Her friend Kona might not regard gum wrappers and ice-cream sticks as treasure. But Stumpy knew the noble dog would not mistake the priceless value of new life in the tall pin oak tree. The tree that for her would be a harbor in a storm. The tree that her own babies would call home.

CHAPTER TWO

Night Talk

"Gwendolyn, are you awake?"

The dog pushed his nose up against the clear glass bowl and looked inside, cross-eyed. It was a cloudy night, and only the warm glow of the gas lamp outside the window gave any light to the room. The Labrador concentrated his attention on the glistening shell lying in the bowl.

"Gwendolyn?"

Scritch. Scrape.

Gwendolyn slowly turned herself around and put

her hermit crab head out to meet the large dark eyes staring in.

"Lovely evening, isn't it, Kona? And nearly a full moon. I can feel it in my bones."

"You have no bones, Gwendolyn," said the Labrador.

"Figure of speech, dear, figure of speech. I expect it's simply the memory of a time when I did. Perhaps I had even more bones than usual. I may have been a hawk in a previous life. Hawks are nothing but bone, I hear."

"Have you been watching public television with Professor Albert again?"

"Well," the old crab said, smiling, *"Amazing Birds of Prey,* if you must know. Personally I'd rather be all tucked up and dreaming of the sea. But Professor Albert is such a dear, and he does love the company."

"I take him to the park," said Kona. "I try to give him company, too."

"You try at everything you do, dear Kona," Gwendolyn answered. "That is why I like you so."

Kona wagged his tail proudly.

Night Talk

"I have some news for you, Gwendolyn," he said.

"Wonderful."

"First, tomorrow should be a high of fifty-two degrees and partly sunny."

"Excellent," said the crab. "So kind of you to watch the evening weather report while I'm napping, dear. So kind. Oh, I do love the weather. I am nearly certain I was a sheep in a past life. Sheep are very weather sensitive, you know."

"I didn't know," said Kona. "And guess what else, Gwendolyn."

Night Talk

"Sunrise at six o'clock," said the crab.

"No," said Kona. "Babies."

"*Babies* at six o'clock?"

"Oh no, just babies," answered the dog. "*Real* babies. Well, not real babies like dog babies. Real babies like *squirrel* babies. Stumpy Squirrel is expecting!"

"You don't say!" answered Gwendolyn.

"Any day now," added Kona.

"Lovely," said Gwendolyn.

"She's building a new nest in a pin oak on the east side of Gooseberry Park. And she's organizing her collection."

"How exciting," said the crab.

"She's dashing about like I've never seen her dash before," Kona continued. "And you know how Stumpy can dash."

"I do," said Gwendolyn. "You've mentioned it many times."

"Yes, I suppose I have," Kona answered. "Every time I see her now, she's running in circles with a mouthful of rubber bands or ice-cream sticks or maple leaves. . . ."

Night Talk

"The nesting instinct," said Gwendolyn, waving a claw in the air. "Happens every time."

Gwendolyn explained to Kona all about the nesting instinct, and as the night lengthened, the two friends talked on. Kona was glad to have Gwendolyn share his excitement about Stumpy's new babies. Kona's favorite animals were squirrels and hermit crabs. He wasn't terribly fond of dogs, though. Dogs could be rude and loud. And leave it to a dog to tell *everyone* your secrets. Squirrels never told secrets. Nor did hermit crabs, especially ones who had been reincarnated seventeen times.

Gwendolyn let Kona dream aloud about the prospect of being an uncle. She smiled with affection as he explained the way he thought young squirrels should be raised. She laughed when he predicted he'd have the children catching a Frisbee between their teeth by July.

Babies were on the way, and it was exciting.

CHAPTER THREE

Friends

Kona had been born in the family room of a fifth-grade teacher on Paradise Lane, Stumpy had been born in a sugar maple near the south entrance of Gooseberry Park, and Gwendolyn had been born in a palm tree on an island somewhere in the Caribbean. It was a miracle that the three had ever found each other.

Of course, this was mostly Professor Albert's doing. He was a retired biology professor who loved to grow daylilies and listen to the saxophone.

Friends

Professor Albert had never married, liked living alone, and all the years he was a professor he never minded the fact that he had no family. He was too busy teaching the cell structures of amphibians.

But after he retired and found himself home so much of the time, he began to grow a little lonely. And when he started talking back to the radio ("Oh yes, *I* love outpatient care, too!"), he realized he needed a pet.

So he bought himself a hermit crab. She was the loveliest of all the crabs in the pet store. Her shell was creamy white with wavy brown lines flowing across it. She was quite big—twice the size of the other crabs—and Professor Albert found her enchanting. So he brought her home from the store in a little paper box, named her Gwendolyn, and became her friend.

Gwendolyn turned out to be a wonderful companion. Professor Albert carried her bowl from room to room in the house, depending on what needed doing. If he was in the kitchen baking banana bread, Gwendolyn was on the kitchen counter. If he was in

Friends

the living room watching television, Gwendolyn was
on the coffee table. If he was writing letters in his
study, Gwendolyn was on the desk.

Professor Albert knew that Gwendolyn liked him
because she always pulled her head far up out of
her shell to look at him when he talked to her.
("Gwendolyn, did you know that each giraffe's mark-
ings are unique?") As the professor spoke, Gwendolyn's delicate antennae moved gracefully back and
forth, and he knew she was listening carefully (having been a teacher, he was quite good at picking out
careful listeners). It was nice, having her.

Friends

Professor Albert was very happy with his hermit crab and he had no plans at all to get a dog. He didn't know he needed a dog. He had never even thought about it.

But one day one of his neighbors who had a sister who had a son in the fifth-grade class of a woman who lived on Paradise Lane told Professor Albert about the teacher's brand-new litter of puppies. Twelve in all. Twelve! The professor could not imagine so many puppies. He tried imagining twelve hermit crabs. So many bowls to carry! How did anyone manage twelve puppies?

His neighbor said that the puppies were chocolate Labradors. Chocolate Labradors! The professor imagined children finding these instead of chocolate rabbits in their Easter baskets. The neighbor said the puppies were round like beach balls and that they loved to play. They played and played and played.

And when Professor Albert heard this, something lit up inside him. Something from when he was a boy. It had to do with dogs and playing.

16

Friends

And before he knew it he was telling his neighbor, "I would like to have one of those puppies."

So Professor Albert found himself in the family room of a fifth-grade teacher on Paradise Lane with twelve fat little puppies running all over him and all over each other and all over everything else in the room. He was delighted and overwhelmed and could hardly catch his breath, and he wondered how he would ever choose just one puppy from so many. They all looked pretty much the same. Should he just pick one up and go?

Friends

But as he was trying to figure all of this out, one of the happy puppies crawled into his lap and stayed. It stayed and stayed and stayed. The other puppies romped across him, licked his face, then ran off somewhere else. But this puppy stayed.

The fifth-grade teacher said to Professor Albert, "Of them all, that's the one who likes to be held the most. He likes company. He'll be glad when he's the only puppy somewhere."

Professor Albert smiled. He knew all about liking company. And this little puppy was staying.

He took the puppy home. He named him Kona, after his favorite coffee. And there in that house Kona grew up.

Friends

Of course, Gwendolyn and Kona became best friends right away. Though Professor Albert couldn't understand Gwendolyn's language, Kona could, and very quickly Gwendolyn assumed the job of puppy training.

"No, Kona dear, you are not allowed to chew Professor Albert's slippers."

"No, Kona dear, dogs do not eat encyclopedias."

"No, Kona dear, you must wait until you are outside to do that. Do you want to go outside? Then sit at the door and bark for Professor Albert. That's right. Bark!"

Kona did everything Gwendolyn told him to do, and Professor Albert said to everyone that raising a puppy was the easiest job in the world. This amused Gwendolyn very much.

Friends

It was a few years more before Kona met the little red squirrel called Stumpy. Gooseberry Park was a very large park with many trees and many more squirrels, and to Kona, of course, all of the squirrels looked alike. Kona went to the park every day with Professor Albert, and while the professor read books about snails and baboons and ants and lilies, listening to Charlie Parker on his Walkman, Kona explored the park and ignored the squirrels.

Then one day as he was exploring, Kona came upon a little red squirrel who was trying to pull a plastic toy tractor up a tree. Holding the tractor in her teeth, the little squirrel pulled it halfway up the tree trunk. But the tractor slipped and crashed to the ground. She ran down to the bottom to start all over again.

Kona walked over to speak to her.

"Perhaps if you pushed it . . . ," he suggested, as the squirrel began pulling at the tractor yet again.

The squirrel opened her mouth. "What?" The tractor crashed.

"Oops," said Kona. "Sorry."

Friends

The little squirrel ran down to try once more.

"It's for my collection," she said to the dog. "I haven't anything this big. Do you know what it's called?"

"A tractor. I've seen them on television," Kona answered.

"Television?" asked the squirrel.

Kona sometimes forgot the world really did have wild animals in it. He couldn't imagine anyone not knowing what a television was.

"Never mind," said Kona. "I simply suggested you push it. Put your paws on the back and roll it up the tree. Just like a boy would."

"Good idea!" said the squirrel. And she pushed the toy tractor all the way up the tree trunk and into her nest. She disappeared inside and was gone for several minutes. Kona started to walk away.

"I'm Stumpy!" The squirrel's little red head popped out of her nest just as the dog was leaving.

"I'm Kona," called the Labrador, happily turning back. "What else do you collect?"

Friends

And that is how Kona met Stumpy. He visited her tree every time Professor Albert took a park bench nap—which was quite often—and from Stumpy he heard tales of life in Gooseberry Park, which he reported back to Gwendolyn, who commented on them as most elderly animals will:

"Leave it to a raccoon to make a mess of things!"

"Oh yes indeed, crows are quite the smart alecks."

"There's nothing like a young possum to warm the heart."

"Thank goodness for rabbits."

These comments Kona took back to Stumpy, and in this way they all became friends.

It was a fine life. A life just right for babies.

CHAPTER FOUR

Murray

It was her first night in her lovely, clean, new nest. Stumpy slept peacefully, feeling the babies move inside her. What a perfectly peaceful . . .

"OUCH!"

Stumpy jumped. Was she dreaming or had someone just yelled "Ouch"? She lay very still and listened. Someone else was definitely in her tree. There was rattling and stumbling above her. Twigs were falling all around. Her first night in the new tree, and here had come a noisy neighbor.

"EXCUSE ME!" yelled Stumpy irritably.

Silence.

"What?" someone called back.

"I said, '*Excuse me,*'" called Stumpy.

"Oh, no problem."

Silence.

"Wait a minute," called the voice. "Was that *sarcasm?*"

Stumpy frowned.

"I'm just trying to get a little sleep here because my babies—"

"BABIES?"

There came a *flum-flum-flum*. Suddenly, perched

on the edge of Stumpy's nest was a tiny black-and-silver bat. He was grinning broadly.

"I *love* babies," he said. He shook Stumpy's paw and peered into her nest.

"So where are they?"

Stumpy, by now, was speechless. Here was a bat in her home in the middle of the night, chatting. She couldn't find her voice, so she simply pointed to her stomach.

"You ate your babies?" asked the bat.

"Who *are* you?" Stumpy finally managed to ask.

The bat grinned and shook Stumpy's paw again.

"Murray," he said. "Name's Murray. And you?"

"Stumpy."

"Pleased to meet you," said the bat. "Did you just move in?"

Stumpy nodded.

"Hey!" Murray said with great cheer. "We'll be neighbors. I've tried every tree in East Gooseberry, and this is the only one that doesn't have a woodpecker living in it. Talk about ruining a neighborhood. Just *you* try to sleep while a woodpecker's having breakfast.

"Speaking of food," said the bat, "have you eaten? Want to go out for Chinese? There's this big green Dumpster over on Sixth that's always full of egg rolls and tasty little packages of duck sauce. Well, tasty if you're not a duck. So, want to go?"

Stumpy looked carefully at the bat.

"You're nocturnal, aren't you?" she asked.

"No way," said Murray. "I'm a Democrat."

"No, no," said Stumpy. "Nocturnal means you sleep all day and stay up all night."

"I knew that," said Murray.

"So?" asked Stumpy.

Murray seemed confused. Then he remembered the question.

"Oh!" he said with relief. "Oh yes. I'm as nocturnal as they come. Do you want to go for Chinese or not?"

Stumpy was very big, very heavy with babies, and also very tired. And she was not nocturnal. She thought it best to stay home. So instead, she invited Murray in for a bite of fresh pita bread she'd found that morning.

Murray

In spite of the rude awakening, Stumpy was happy for Murray's company. She sensed that her babies were due to arrive very soon, and it was good having him to talk to. She didn't feel lonely or afraid. Murray told her all about his cousin Rudy's sinus problems and his great-aunt Miriam's bad knee and the heart palpitations that ran in his family.

He also told her about the fall he'd had as a young bat, when he was hanging from a tree by one foot and trying to unwrap a Mars bar with the other. He had gotten so excited that he slipped and hit the ground headfirst. Since then he'd had some problems with his echolocation and couldn't seem to fly in the dark without bumping into things.

Murray

"You'd think I'd manage not to bump into my own tree," said Murray sheepishly. "But I do. All the time."

"How long have you lived in Gooseberry Park?" asked Stumpy.

"Oh, all my life," said Murray. "I was born on the North Side into a big family. Four girls and a boy. My sisters are crazy about music, so they moved into town over a store called the Vinyl Nightmare. And my parents retired to Disneyland. They're living in one of those houses in It's a Small World. So now it's just me. I tried to fix the old place up after my folks left, but it was too big a job. Lots of shag carpeting. My mother loved shag carpet. In our living room—"

"You had a living room?" asked Stumpy.

"Oh sure," said Murray. "It was a split-level. And how about you?"

"Well, I collect things," said Stumpy.

"Yeah?"

"Yes, I—OH!" Stumpy grabbed her stomach.

"Pardon?" Murray said.

"OH!" Stumpy cried out again.

Murray's eyes grew large.

"Indigestion?" he asked. ". . . Or babies?"

"I think I need to be alone now," Stumpy said, still holding her stomach.

Murray jumped up.

"Absolutely!" he said. "I've got a million things to do anyway. Empty the garbage, water my plants, floss. I am *out* of here."

He perched on the edge of the nest, then looked back at Stumpy, worried.

"If you need me, just yell. I'm only one flight up."

Stumpy smiled.

"Good night, Murray. I'll be fine. I'll call you in the morning."

The tiny bat grinned.

"Babies!" he said. Then he was gone.

Alone, Stumpy swept away the remaining pita crumbs, then curled herself into a warm corner of the nest where she had made a special bed of sweet-smelling pine needles. She closed her eyes and took several deep breaths.

"So how many ducks do you think it *takes* to make one of those little packages of sauce?" called a voice from above.

Stumpy smiled.

CHAPTER FIVE

Time

"Kona," Gwendolyn whispered into the darkness. "It's begun."

The dog lifted his large brown head from his bed in the corner of the living room.

"Listen," said Gwendolyn.

Kona held himself quite still and listened. There was the ticking of the Swiss clock on the mantel. The hush of warm air from the gas fireplace. The subtle buzz of the plant light above Professor Albert's violets. And . . . something else.

Time

"Can you feel it in the air, Kona?" Gwendolyn shifted her shell around to look at him directly.

Kona waited, and as he did, a most powerful feeling came over him.

"Is it Stumpy?" he whispered. "Is it time?"

The old crab stretched her antennae as high as they could reach. She searched the air.

"I believe it is time," she said with conviction.

Oh." Kona jumped up. "Oh."

He went to the picture window and looked out toward the tops of the trees in Gooseberry Park.

"I wish I could be there," he said. He rested his front paws upon the windowsill.

"Kona dear," said Gwendolyn, "you are a most remarkable dog. But, I am sorry to say, not so remarkable as to climb a tree and assist a squirrel having babies."

"I wish I were," Kona said with a sigh. "I wish I were that remarkable."

"She'll be fine, dear," Gwendolyn said reassuringly, fully believing this herself. "She's a plucky one."

Kona stared out toward the park a while longer,

Time

then he began to pace. He went from the living room to the dining room, turned right at the sideboard to the study, circled the study, then paced back to the living room exactly the way he'd come. He longed for a good bone to chew, but he'd left his best one in the backyard. He plopped down on the floor and began chewing the leg of the coffee table.

"Kona!" yelled Gwendolyn.

"What?!" The dog jumped so fast that he banged

his nose on the table. "Thanks, Gwendolyn. Forgot where I was. I don't think there's much damage."

The old crab shook her head.

"Kona, my dear, there are some things in this life we must experience alone."

"Even having babies?" asked Kona.

"Even having babies," answered Gwendolyn. "Why, when I had my children—"

"Gwendolyn, *you* have children?" Kona's eyes were wide with surprise.

The crab smiled.

"Dear, I had quite a full life in the tropics before I was carried off to be sold in a pet shop. Not that I'm complaining, mind you. I am very devoted to our Professor Albert."

Time

"Children?" asked Kona.

"At least fifty," answered Gwendolyn. "All grown now. And let me tell you, my friend, giving birth is something very private, and rather sacred. It was, for me, as private as prayer."

"Oh," said Kona with a solemn look on his face.

Together the two gazed out the window in silence, at the trees, the stars, the clear bright moon in the sky. Each was full of thoughts: thoughts about the earth and its heavens, about mothers and their children, about the profound comfort of shelter and sustenance and the familiarity of home. And both sent forth their best, their strongest, their most sustaining thoughts to a little red squirrel who, at that very moment, was happily nursing two baby boys and one baby girl in the good green fragrance of a pin oak tree.

CHAPTER SIX

Children

The following several days were rather heady ones for the little red squirrel who had become a mother. Never had she received so much attention and praise. Never had she been so talked about. The birth of new babies is important news anywhere, and Gooseberry Park was no exception. Word spread quickly through the trees and burrows and along the riverbank that triplets had been born to the busy red squirrel who collected yogurt cups. Friends Stumpy hadn't seen in months suddenly dropped by, carrying gifts of hard, pungent walnuts or choice bits of ham sandwich or the occasional french fry, which was considered quite a delicacy in park circles. Red, gray, and black squirrels oohed and aahed. Mourning doves cooed, starlings cackled, and cardinals peeked shyly over the edge of the nest. Even a fat old possum hoisted himself up the tree to pay his respects.

A brisk, cold wind was blowing now, unusual for early April. The park was strangely quiet as the trees leaned into the chilly breezes. But Stumpy had no worries. She had three beautiful babies, a fine collection of treasures, and a wonderful new neighbor who loved bringing her egg rolls. The winds could blow as hard as they might. She was secure.

Kona, of course, had been by to visit every day since the babies' arrival. He still hadn't met Murray, since the bat slept most of the day. And, of course, Kona hadn't met Stumpy's children yet, either. They were much too tiny to be carried down to the ground. But Stumpy herself came down when Kona called

Children

her name, and she told him all the wonderful details. She said the little girl loved to sleep and that she sang in her sleep like a little bird. The two baby boy squirrels liked to rest on each other, and one preferred the bottom and one preferred the top, so she had named them Top and Bottom. The little girl was called Sparrow for her pretty songs. Their eyes weren't even open yet.

Stumpy said it was hard work, being a mother to newborns. She couldn't waste time or explore for fun anymore. Whenever she left the nest, it was only to pull a few pinecones from a tree stump or to unearth a few acorns buried nearby. Then she had to hurry back home, for her babies would be waking and crying to be fed. She had never felt so needed. She had never felt so tired.

Children

Still, she told Kona, she had never felt so happy. And Murray visited every night.

Kona trotted cheerfully back home and reported to Gwendolyn, word for word, everything Stumpy had told him. Though Gwendolyn had never met Stumpy personally, she regarded the squirrel as an old friend, and she was glad for the good news from Kona. Glad for the babies in Gooseberry Park.

CHAPTER SEVEN

Ice

New babies alone cannot change the designs of fate, and no one knew, not even Gwendolyn, the drama that lay just ahead for Stumpy and for all of the animals in Gooseberry Park. The park had known its share of danger. The animals had lived through drought and the specter of a dying river. They had watched a tornado take a few trees from the South Side one spring. There had been deep snow and lightning and the threat of a boy with an air rifle.

I c e

But what they were about to face was a danger none of them could have imagined.

When just before dawn the freezing rain began to fall, Gwendolyn, looking out Professor Albert's window, knew that a day of trouble had arrived. Morning came, and the steady *pick pick pick* of icy pellets against the house kept Professor Albert and Kona and Gwendolyn at the window, their faces full of concern. And as the day wore on and the ice thickened, the earth all around them began to suffer.

Ice dropped from the sky and covered everything. It coated houses, swing sets, streetlights, telephone wires. It encased picnic tables, cars, fences, trains. And it froze trees. The trees were first wet and cold and slick. Then the slickness hardened and became ice. And the ice grew thicker and thicker and heavier and heavier, and soon the trees began to bow their weary limbs until finally the limbs snapped, crashing to the ground. The sap froze in other trees and exploded with a sound like gunpowder as they fell.

Professor Albert had just planted a pink dogwood and a small flowering crab apple and a gingko tree.

I c e

All three were too young to withstand the assault of the ice, and during the course of the afternoon they dropped, one by one. Professor Albert had tried to run out and throw a quilt over the gingko, but he fell down his front steps and slid all the way to the mailbox. Kona stood at the door and barked and barked.

The professor hobbled back into his house, muttering that he should have moved to Florida with all of the other retired professors. He fixed himself a cup of hot Darjeeling tea, then, and, sore and ex-

I c e

hausted, promptly went to sleep. He slept so soundly, tucked under a knitted throw on his living room sofa, that even the loudest snap of falling branches didn't stir him. Kona and Gwendolyn were left to do all of the worrying.

And, of course, it was not the fate of gingko trees that had them knotted up inside. It was the fate of their small squirrel friend and her newborn children.

No one could have guessed which trees in Gooseberry Park would stand through the storm and which trees would fall. No one could have guessed that an old ash tree over by the river would bend and groan and suffer under the weight of the ice, but would hold steady. And that other stronger, sturdier trees —oak trees—would break.

When the storm began, Stumpy had burrowed herself and her babies under the thick blanket of twigs and leaves in her nest to keep dry, as she always did in a rain. And when the rain had become ice, persistently tapping against the leaf blanket, still Stumpy had not been afraid. She had endured sleet, and a little fine ice on the trees was no worry to her.

Ice

But when the leaf blanket grew heavier and heavier with its freezing weight, and a deep, cold chill that she could not warm began to run through Stumpy's body, and as the air filled with the groans and agonizing cracks of trees falling under, the little red squirrel became very, very afraid. Had she been alone, she would have fled her nest and gone to a safe underground burrow.

But Stumpy was not alone. She had three babies, babies whose eyes were barely open and whose bodies were still pink in places where the fur had not yet grown in, babies who could not be moved in a deluge of icy rain without great risk.

Stumpy drew the three babies more tightly under her body and tried to calm their whimperings each time a dying tree cracked like thunder on its way down. She wondered how Murray was, if he was as frightened as she, if he also was wishing for the comfort of company. Under the weight of the ice, she could not call to him. She hoped he was safe wherever he was, and she tried to cheer herself up by imagining him trapped in the Chinese Dumpster, under the ice with a week's worth of egg rolls. And it was when she was thinking of him, and smiling to herself, that a kind of explosion sounded in her ears, and her world lost its balance and went falling, falling to the cold, hard ground.

CHAPTER EIGHT

A Very Big Risk

When evening descended and the ice storm had stopped, the professor still slept while Kona kept vigil at the window, trembling as giant pines bent their icy heads to the ground and jumping at the sharp sounds of thick bark breaking. All of the lights in the neighborhood were out. The refrigerator didn't hum, the plant light didn't buzz, and the warm furnace air didn't hush through the vents. Professor Albert's fireplace and the gas post lamp in the front yard were the only sources of light, and they cast a funereal glow upon the house and its occupants, stranded like polar bears on an arctic floe.

A Very Big Risk

"What are we going to do, Gwendolyn?" Kona asked, his big head casting a giant shadow over her bowl. "Stumpy is in serious trouble."

"Yes," Gwendolyn answered, nodding. "It's serious, very serious. Even if her tree is still standing, she will be trapped in her nest. And the ice . . . the babies . . ."

"I have to help her," Kona said, pacing in circles around the living room.

"Kona dear, what can you do? She is at the top of a tall tree. There would be no way of reaching her. And the journey to the park—treacherous, very treacherous indeed. The ice is difficult—nearly impossible—to cross, as poor Professor Albert demonstrated earlier. Trees are coming down, heavy branches dropping from great heights. Kona, you would be taking a very big risk. And perhaps for naught. She is over a hundred feet in the air."

"What if she isn't, Gwendolyn?" Kona stopped pacing and looked at the crab. "What if her tree is one of those that came down?"

Gwendolyn shook her head sadly.

A Very Big Risk

"If it was, then I very much doubt, dear, that Stumpy . . . such a fall . . ."

The old crab looked at the dog and spoke gently, "Her chance of surviving seems very unlikely."

Kona took a deep breath and, with eyes wide and sincere, answered, "Whether she is alive or not, Gwendolyn, I have to take care of her."

The crab sighed.

"Well, my dear, I expect you do, I expect you do. But I am not sure how you will accomplish it."

Five minutes later, Gwendolyn was working the lock on Professor Albert's front door.

A Very Big Risk

Kona held her steadily in his mouth, and with a deft claw she turned the mechanism gently, gently, then *click*. It was done.

Kona placed her back in her bowl.

"Thank you for not sneezing, dear," she said.

"I'm still not sure if I can get the door open," said Kona.

"Just pretend the knob is a bone," Gwendolyn answered. "I have every confidence you will do it."

And the dog did. After only a minute or so of vigorous gnawing and biting, the door popped open.

A Very Big Risk

Kona looked back at his good friend staring anxiously through the glass, at Professor Albert snoring peacefully on the sofa, at his own warm bed in the corner, and at the inviting flames of the fireplace.

"I'll be back soon, Gwendolyn," he said.

"Of course you will," said the crab. "Take good care, dear." She did not want Kona to know how worried she was.

When Kona went out the front door, he didn't close it all the way behind him. He needed to be able to get back into the house before Professor Albert woke again. Kona breathed deeply, took one strong, confident step, and with a magnificent slide, shot right off Professor Albert's porch into the top of a juniper bush.

Sprawled there, he groaned and looked out at the several blocks he would have to cross to reach Gooseberry Park. He looked back at Gwendolyn in the window, her antennae swirling around and around. Just then a heavy branch from a tree across the street crashed into his neighbor's front yard, taking several broken shingles with it.

A Very Big Risk

Kona sighed, then carefully maneuvered back onto his feet. Inching his way slowly, he began his icy journey. Gooseberry Park seemed to him to be on the other side of the world.

Instead of taking the sidewalk, Kona decided to cut through yards. It would save time, and there would be more things to hold on to. He crossed one yard by hanging on to a hemlock hedge. A second yard had a rail fence he steadied himself against. In another, a long concrete planter kept him on his feet.

Some yards had nothing at all to hold on to except the occasional ice-covered bush. In these yards Kona danced, skated, skied, and rolled. He fell again and again, and once he struck his nose so hard that it bled. Kona saw not one sign of life along the way, save

A Very Big Risk

for a large yellow tomcat who tried to impress him by strolling easily across the icy top of an Oldsmobile. Kona gave him a sour look and went on.

The dog's body was bruised and his spirits had taken a beating as well, but he was determined. He knew where to find Stumpy's tree and he was bound to make it there. Something inside was telling him to do this. His teeth ached from holding on to every solid object he could grasp, and his tongue was numb with cold.

But something called him. And no matter the price, he would answer.

CHAPTER NINE

Rescue and Remorse

When he finally reached Stumpy's pin oak tree, Kona was stunned by what he saw. The top of the tree had been snapped off like a bean. What was left of its lower trunk still stood sharp and upright, ice hanging down its sides like a fresh-cut wound. Scattered across the ground lay the debris that had once given the giant oak its majesty: solid pieces of trunk, mammoth branches with long, graceful stems, hundreds of broken twigs—all glistening under a hard layer of ice. Kona could barely breathe.

53

Rescue and Remorse

For a moment he simply closed his eyes.

Then he whispered, "Stumpy?"

His voice was lost in the desolation of the park.

He cleared his throat and this time spoke louder, "Stumpy?"

Clamping his teeth on to the scattered branches to steady himself, he made his way around what was left of the tree. Every few feet he called out "Stumpy?" Each time he was met by silence. And when he found a part of Stumpy's nest scattered on the ground, bits of bright material and gum wrappers thrown everywhere, it was almost more than he could bear. He sat down and hung his head.

Rescue and Remorse

Stopped there, motionless, discouraged, confused, and very cold, Kona heard a sound. It was a sound like a song. He lifted his ears. The sound was coming from within a large piece of broken trunk that had rolled away from the rest of the debris and settled against a broad rhododendron bush. Kona stood up and listened more intently.

"Rock-a-bye Bottom in the tree Top!" someone sang. "Get it?"

R e s c u e a n d R e m o r s e

"Stump!" Kona's voice boomed across the wreckage. "Stump!"

The dog leaped forward then danced like a Bolshevik until he landed beside the singing tree trunk, flat on his back. He moaned. From a small round hole in the trunk, a little black head fuzzed with silver poked out. It looked at Kona.

"Help!" the head shouted.

Kona raised himself up and moved closer. The little black head that had yelled for help belonged to a bat.

"Murray?" he inquired.

"In person!" answered the bat.

"Are you all right?" Kona asked.

"I think we bounced," said Murray. "You must be

Kona. I knew Stumpy would find you. The kids are all in here, snoring like elephants."

"Stumpy didn't find me," said Kona. "I came on my own."

"You did?" asked Murray. "Stumpy's not with you?"

"No," said Kona.

"Well she's not with *me!*" wailed Murray. "She said she'd go get *you!*"

"WHERE IS SHE?" the two said together.

Kona's heart sank. He looked all around the deathly quiet park.

"Stump!" he called. "Stump!"

"Oh, woe," said Murray, shaking his head. "She said she'd find you and you could help us. Now she's disappeared. Oh, woe."

One of the babies inside the hole began to cry. Another sneezed.

"These kids are freezing," said Murray. He went back inside the hole to wrap them in his wings.

Kona was torn. He had to look for Stumpy, but where had she gone? She had never been to his house, so how did she think she would find him? The fall must have rattled her senses. Kona wanted to keep looking for her, but the babies needed shelter—and quickly. It would be very dangerous for them to be exposed to the cold much longer.

Kona made his decision. He spoke into the hole.

"We have to get you to my house, Murray. You and the babies. Then I'll come back to search for Stumpy."

"Me and the babies?" Murray said from within. "Me? I'll be OK."

"I can't get them out of here alone," said Kona.

"Can't you just call a cab or something?"

Kona was thinking hard.

"I've got it," he said. "You can all ride on my back."

"Excuse me?" said Murray. He popped his head out of the hole again.

"It's the only way," Kona insisted. "You can sit on my back and tuck the children inside your wings. It will be like riding a horse."

"Sure, like I've ever ridden a horse," answered

Murray. "We're gonna end up on *Hard Copy*. I know it."

But within minutes, Murray was on Kona's back, humming nervously, the babies tucked under his wings.

Now that Kona had to carry everyone, he was really worried. He had fallen dozens of times on his way to the park, but he couldn't risk any such accidents on the journey home. There was only one thing to do.

"What?" Murray called out. "We're *crawling?* We're going to *crawl?* Gee, maybe we'll get there by September!"

"We'll make it," said Kona. "Just hold tight to those babies."

"Ouch!" Murray yelled. "Ouch! Doesn't Stumpy ever feed these kids?"

It took Kona an hour and a half to make what was usually a ten-minute walk to his house. It was a good thing he was a Labrador retriever. Labradors can withstand very cold temperatures and great pain, and only a dog like Kona could have made the

grueling journey home. In the moonlight of the clearing sky, everything glittered like diamonds, as if all the world had become a jewel, and even as Kona pulled himself across the yards, he was moved and strengthened by the incredible beauty all around him. He might even have forgotten that the others were with him had not Murray yelled "Giddyap!" every five minutes.

Rescue and Remorse

When Kona finally saw Professor Albert's house again and saw that the front door was still slightly ajar and that the fireplace still glowed and that he was home, he wanted to weep. It was as if he were gazing at heaven itself.

When Kona turned into the yard, Murray knew, too, that they had arrived.

"Yippee!" he yelled.

Kona struggled up the icy steps, then cautiously put his head inside the door. Professor Albert still lay snoring on the sofa.

"Welcome back, dear," Gwendolyn said softly.

Kona walked into the room and gently lay down on the floor. Murray scooped the babies up and hopped off.

"Wow," said Murray. "Look at the size of that television! Did I tell you I love *Jeopardy?*"

Gwendolyn smiled at Kona.

"A remarkable dog," she said.

CHAPTER TEN

The Wanderer

When Professor Albert finally woke up, it was four o'clock in the morning. Gwendolyn was waving her antennae like an inspired conductor; Kona could be heard rattling around down in the basement; some little bits of . . . egg roll? . . . lay on the carpet; and the world outside was nothing but solid, unyielding ice. It was too much for an old biology professor. He refilled Kona's dish, handed Gwendolyn a piece of broccoli, put on an extra pair of socks, and went straight to his bedroom. Professor Albert had never been an amateur when it came to sleeping. Years of standing beside philosophy majors trying to label the insides of frogs had taught him the fine art of turning off his brain whenever he wished. So he turned it off and went back to sleep.

Down in the basement, Kona was trying to settle his houseguests into a giant box of Christmas decorations.

"This is embarrassing," said Kona, plumping a Christmas tree skirt around the babies with a gentle paw. "Ordinarily I'd put you in the guest room—very nice, its own bath—but I don't think we could count on a hearty welcome from Professor Albert. Once a chipmunk wandered in and he chased it for two hours with a colander."

"He cooks Italian?" said Murray.

Kona smiled and turned to leave.

"I hope you find Stumpy," Murray said suddenly, solemnly.

Kona nodded and looked again at the three sleeping children.

The Wanderer

"Now that the professor is in his bedroom, I'll be able to go to the park again," Kona said. "I'll toss down a bag of marshmallows before I go. Then I'll get some real food for you when I get back."

"Marshmallows are real food," said Murray, perking up.

"Wish me luck, Murray," Kona said, quickly going up the stairs.

It was a painful run back to the park. Kona's cuts stung badly in the cold. The pads of his feet hurt from the ice's abrasion. And his entire body ached.

But the dog made it back to the park, and this time more quickly. He was afraid Stumpy might be

The Wanderer

injured and hurting somewhere. There was no time to waste thinking of his own bumps and bruises.

A few of the animals in Gooseberry Park had begun to emerge from the wreckage. They wandered slowly in the moonlight. A large black crow flew low overhead, surveying the sight.

"Have you seen a little red squirrel?" Kona called to the crow.

"A girl?" asked the crow.

"No, no. A squirrel. A little red one." Kona waited as the crow landed beside him.

"A squirrel, you say?" asked the crow.

"Yes," said Kona.

"Red?"

"Yes."

"About this big?" asked the crow, opening his wings.

"Yes, yes!" Kona cried excitedly.

"No," the crow said.

"No?" repeated Kona.

The crow spread his enormous wings and left.

"Gwendolyn was right," Kona muttered to himself as the bird disappeared. "Crows really *are* smart alecks."

Kona sniffed all around the fallen pin oak. It was difficult to catch a good scent, with the ground so frozen and so much of Stumpy's home scattered.

A possum limped past. Her ear was bleeding.

"I've lost my boy!" she said to Kona. "Have you seen my boy?"

"No. I'm sorry," Kona replied with concern.

"Mama!" a voice cried out from a nearby spruce.

The possum gasped. "He's there! I'm coming, dear, I'm coming!"

Kona smiled and watched as the mother possum made her way across the ice to her son. A small gray shape slipped down the trunk of the spruce and leaped onto her back.

Watching them leave, Kona felt a heavy sadness.

Turning, he called, "Stumpy! Stumpy!"

"Whoo?" a voice asked from the branches of a fallen walnut tree. "Whoo?" it asked again.

Kona saw two large yellow eyes peering at him through the branches.

"Stumpy, the little red squirrel," Kona answered. "Do you know her?"

The owl lifted himself up and flew nearer Kona.

"I certainly do," said the owl. "She has those

babies with the strange names. What are they . . . Up? Down?"

"Top and Bottom," Kona answered. "And Sparrow, the little girl."

"Oh yes, lovely children." The owl suddenly winced with pain.

"Are you all right?" Kona asked in alarm.

"Thank you, yes. Just a twist in the neck from the fall. I was eating dinner when my tree went down. Paying no attention whatever. It hit before I knew what was happening."

"Did you see Stumpy? Have you seen her since the storm?"

"I heard her," the owl said.

"Heard her? Where? When?"

"I am not certain when," said the owl. "The evening is a bit of a blur, you know. But I heard her. She was saying, 'I have to find Paradise Lane.'"

"Oh, my goodness!" exclaimed Kona. "She's looking for me, and she's completely confused! Paradise Lane is where I was born, not where I live now! My home is on Miller Street!"

The Wanderer

"Oh, my," said the owl. "That is nowhere near Paradise Lane."

"I know, I know!" cried the dog. "If she's headed to Paradise Lane, she'll never find me! And how will I ever find her?"

The owl began to shake his head. This took a while, of course. When an owl shakes his head, he first must turn it very, very slowly to the far, far left.

The Wanderer

He must then turn it very, very slowly to the far, far right. Kona was amazed as he watched.

The owl winced again.

"Your neck," said Kona.

"Yes," said the owl.

"But why did you shake your head?" asked Kona.

"Because you will not be able to find her," said the owl.

"But I have to!"

"She is wandering, my boy, and no one can find a wanderer. The wanderer must first find you."

Kona sighed with frustration.

"Stumpy isn't very smart. She doesn't even know what a television is."

"A what?" asked the owl.

"Never mind," Kona said glumly. "My feet are frozen and there are three babies and a bat in the Christmas ornaments, and then Professor Albert's marshmallows—"

"Snap out of it, son!" the owl grumbled. "Go on home now. You're babbling."

Kona turned to go back home.

The Wanderer

"And where are all of her yogurt cups?" he said. "And the rubber bands . . . Did Murray say he's *Italian?*"

The owl sat and stared as the large weary Labrador mumbled and slipped his way across the ice, heading back to his home on Miller Street, wishing it were Paradise.

CHAPTER ELEVEN

Guests

Later that morning Murray rubbed his eyes, stretched his wings, and gave a giant yawn. Top, Bottom, and Sparrow were all sleeping soundly against him. And Kona was coming down the stairs.

Murray grinned and waved at the dog.

"Say, Kona! What's for breakfast?"

"Breakfast?" said the dog. "You want breakfast?"

Murray nodded.

"Murray, when I got back from Gooseberry Park this morning at six, you ate a whole bag of Fritos, a box of Ritz crackers, a sixteen-ounce package of provolone cheese, and an orange."

"I ate an orange?" Murray asked.

"It's only ten. How in the world can you still be hungry?" said the dog.

"I *never* eat oranges," Murray said.

"How can you even move?" Kona asked.

"They make me break out," said the bat.

Murray looked down at the pile of sleeping babies.

"Hi, gang," he said. "Want a Pop-Tart?"

"Just wait here," said Kona. "I'll bring something down soon. The pudding cup seemed to be all right for the babies last night, so I'll try to steal another one for them. But you have to stay here and keep quiet, Murray. We can't let Professor Albert find you."

"Sure," answered Murray cheerfully. "No problem. But . . . what are my chances of getting a Mars bar?"

"Just *stay*," said Kona, disappearing back up the stairs.

Guests

Murray sighed. He looked all around the basement. Pipes. Wires. What to do?

Suddenly the sound of a television show came drifting down.

"*Jeopardy!*" cried Murray. "My favorite!"

He jumped out of the box, ready to dash upstairs. Then he remembered Kona's instruction: *Stay.*

Murray walked in circles around and around the box, hearing the familiar theme song float down from above.

"Oh-oh-oh-oh-oh-oh," said Murray, trying hard to stay. Trying *really* hard to stay.

"But Alex Trebek is my idol!" he wailed. And, *flum-flum-flum,* he was on his way.

The basement steps led to the kitchen. Murray flew in and, hiding inside a china cabinet, poked his head out and looked toward the living room. Professor Albert was watching television and eating a Danish. Kona sat beside him, looking rather impatient and glancing often toward the basement. Kona didn't see Murray in the cabinet.

"And now we'll begin our round of Double Jeopardy," said Alex Trebek.

Guests

Murray sighed with pleasure and settled down to watch.

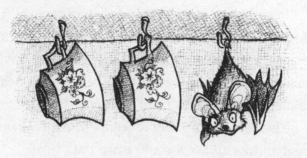

Soon, however, the sight and smell of Professor Albert's Danish was just too much for the tiny bat. He was hungry. He needed breakfast.

Murray's nose went up in the air, sniffing, sniffing.

"Hmmm," said the little bat to himself. "Now where would a professor keep a Danish?"

He flew to the top of the cabinet and looked out over the confusion of Professor Albert's kitchen counters.

"A bottle of vitamin C. Bottle of vitamin A. Bottle of vitamin E. Gee, I'm watering at the mouth." His eyes searched a different counter.

"Wheat germ. Olive oil. Soybean curd—oh, *gross!* Maple granola. Oreos. Lima beans . . . OREOS!"

Guests

Murray jumped so hard he hit his head on the ceiling. *Thump!*

In the living room Kona pricked up his ears. The dog looked toward the kitchen and saw Murray hopping up and down on top of the china cabinet, waving to him and pointing to something below. Kona nearly fainted. He shook his head fiercely at Murray.

The bat mouthed some words to him. "Creamy center" was all Kona could make out.

The Labrador frowned and firmly shook his head again. He had to wait for Professor Albert to take a morning nap before carrying any more food to the basement. The professor would likely be home all day, with the ice outside still so thick. They were lucky even to have the electricity back on.

And Murray was supposed to be staying in the basement, but there he was, bouncing like a ball on the china cabinet.

Murray *had* to behave. Kona vigorously shook his head at the bat again.

"A flea, Kona?" the professor asked, putting down his Danish and rubbing Kona's ears.

"No, just a *pest,*" the Labrador said to himself.

Back in the kitchen, Murray threw up his wings in exasperation.

"A whole bag of Oreos in the kitchen, and the dog only wants his ears scratched. Domestic animals—who can figure 'em?"

Flum. Murray dropped down to the kitchen counter.

Just then Professor Albert rose and said something about needing some butter.

"Uh-oh," said Murray, who was just getting to his first creamy center.

Professor Albert started for the kitchen.

"Double uh-oh!" Murray said again, stuffing the Oreo in his mouth and looking for a place to hide.

The professor took a few more steps toward the kitchen. But before he could get there—

CRASH!

"What?!" The professor spun around.

On the living room floor Professor Albert's Chinese ginger jar lamp lay in a hundred pieces. Kona sat very still and wagged his tail. Just a bit.

G u e s t s

Murray seized his opportunity. The cookie still in his mouth, he grabbed two more with his feet and flew down the basement steps.

Back in the living room, Professor Albert was saying that he didn't understand how a lamp could just knock itself off a table and why did he keep thinking he heard a bird in the house and, really, weren't the past twenty-four hours the strangest anyone had ever seen?

Kona, glancing over at the sleeping Gwendolyn, tried to wipe the guilty look off his face. He could not have agreed more with the old professor.

Chapter Twelve

Food and Conversation

For the next few days while Kona and Gwendolyn tried to figure out how to find Stumpy, bags of nacho chips, boxes of after dinner mints, jars of crunchy peanut butter, and the occasional chocolate bar with almonds kept disappearing mysteriously from the kitchen. Poor Professor Albert. He would stand in front of the refrigerator or in front of the pantry, scratching his head in confusion. He would tell himself that he was *not* getting senile, that he just *thought* he'd bought that bag of chips or that jar of peanut butter. No cans of lima beans or spinach ever

Food and Conversation

disappeared. It was as if some force in the universe wanted Professor Albert to eat only healthy things. And he still couldn't figure out why Kona was so nervous every time they watched *Jeopardy.* Things certainly had seemed odd since that ice storm.

But Professor Albert's problems were nothing compared to Kona's. The dog was constantly going through the house picking up empty potato chip bags or candy wrappers. If Professor Albert found these, he would surely think that Kona was the one taking his food. And Kona certainly was *not* the one.

"You have to clean up after yourself, Murray," Kona would say to the bat.

"Oh, sorry, Kona," Murray would answer. "But I was watching *Days of Our Lives* through the heat vent and I was so upset about Daniel and Laura that I forgot those Milky Way wrappers. Daniel is such a rat!"

Still, in spite of his hectic life and his worries about Stumpy, Kona was enjoying having Murray and the babies at his house. And late night was the best time of all.

Food and Conversation

Long after Professor Albert had gone off to bed—complaining again that he just couldn't understand where an entire bag of Chips Ahoy could disappear to and speculating that another of those pesky chipmunks was sneaking in—Kona, finally able to relax, would softly pad over to Gwendolyn's bowl, pick her up gently in his mouth, and the two would sneak down into the basement.

Murray, being nocturnal, was always wide awake and usually swinging by his feet somewhere. When Kona and Gwendolyn appeared, he would do a little somersault and land with his wings outspread.

"Ta-da!" he'd sing. "So, who's got the Pepsi?"

Top, Bottom, and Sparrow would lift their little heads and look up from the box at Gwendolyn.

"Oh dear, oh dear! Such pretty babies!" the crab would fuss. "Such chubby little legs! And is that a tooth you have, Mister Bottom?" Gwendolyn's antennae moved wildly in the air.

Kona beamed with joy. He loved the babies, too.

Then the friends would all gather in and around the box in the quiet night. Murray told vampire

Food and Conversation

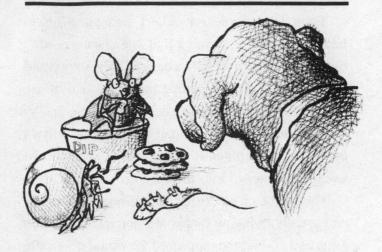

jokes ("Why do vampires brush their teeth in the morning?" "To fight bat breath!"); Gwendolyn read everyone's palm; and Kona told them again the story of his icy journey to Gooseberry Park. They all loved to hear it.

When Kona told them about the cat who strolled

across the Oldsmobile, Murray said, "I know that cat. His name is Conroy. He eats Chinese, too. Plus French. Italian. Canadian. Anybody will do!" The bat cracked up over his joke.

And at times they were serious and wistful.

"Do you think she'll find us?" Kona asked.

"I am certain of it, dear," Gwendolyn answered. "I can feel it in my bones."

"You have bones?" Murray asked the crab.

"Figure of speech, Murray," said Kona. "Figure of speech."

And after an hour or two of good food and conversation, Kona began to yawn.

"How can you be sleepy?" Murray asked. "It's only three o'clock"

"Even I am a bit drowsy," Gwendolyn said, smiling at the bat. "I think it may be due to all of this lovely food you provided." She gestured to the graham crackers, the raisin bread, the banana chips scattered about.

"We didn't even get to the pretzels and bean dip yet," said Murray.

Food and Conversation

Kona and Gwendolyn bade their friend good night, kissed the babies, and returned quietly upstairs. Kona eased Gwendolyn down into her bowl, then looked at her through the glass. Each night he said the same thing: "I hope Stumpy finds us."

And each night Gwendolyn's answer was the same: "She will."

CHAPTER THIRTEEN

The Weasel

It was several days after the ice storm before Professor Albert took Kona to Gooseberry Park again. First they had to wait for warmer air to blow in and the ice to melt. Then they had to wait for park crews to remove the devastation of fallen trees. The sound of chain saws filled the air, leaving everyone in Professor Albert's house with a heavy heart. Particularly Kona. He thought of Stumpy's cozy nest

The Weasel

destroyed, all her treasures scattered and gone. And he wondered if he really would ever see her again.

Finally Professor Albert resumed his walks to the park, and Kona was mightily relieved, for he had hopes of hearing news there of Stumpy. With the warmer weather, many animals would be out. Someone was bound to know something.

When he arrived at Gooseberry Park, Kona could not help his hopes sinking a little. Nearly every tree had suffered some injury, and many had not survived at all. Large piles of sawed trunks and branches lay everywhere. The remains of Stumpy's beautiful pin oak were among them.

Still, Kona could sense in the air a spirit of renewal around him. The animals were stirring. There was life. There was hope.

While Professor Albert read a book on clams, Kona took off to look for clues to Stumpy's whereabouts. He stopped to chat with a chipmunk who had just awakened from hibernation and was still a little groggy.

"Are you acquainted with a squirrel named Stumpy?" Kona asked.

The Weasel

The chipmunk yawned. "Whose cabbage was it?" he said.

Kona sighed and moved on.

Then Kona met a mallard duck who said that no, he didn't know what had become of Stumpy, but that the weasels on the West Side were bound to know something. All weasels lived for gossip and sensational events. And if one weasel knew something, *all* weasels knew it.

Kona thanked the mallard and headed across the park.

Once he arrived on the West Side, it didn't take Kona long to find a weasel. He simply stood on a tree stump and said as loudly as he could, "What a *strange story!*" And sure enough, from behind a broken maple a weasel popped out his head.

The weasel ran over to Kona, sniffing the air.

"What's strange?" the weasel asked. "What? What?"

"It's about that squirrel who lost her babies over on the East Side."

"Yeah, I heard about that squirrel," answered the weasel. "So what?"

The Weasel

"Well," Kona replied confidentially, "I hear that a dog on Miller Street . . . Do you know Miller Street?"

"Yeah, I know it! I know it! Go on!" said the weasel.

"Well," Kona continued, "a dog on Miller Street has some treasure that belongs to that squirrel, but he can't find her anywhere. And he actually wants to give the treasure *back*. Now, isn't that strange?"

"The dog lives on Miller Street, you say?" asked the weasel.

"Right," said Kona, thinking as fast as he could. "And I hear he's planning to put a sign on his house tomorrow night. So the squirrel can find him."

The Weasel

"What kind of sign?" asked the weasel. "Like, WELCOME SQUIRREL or something?"

"No. I hear that it's going to be a sign only the squirrel will know. A secret sign," Kona answered. "Imagine. Leading straight to treasure!"

"You sure it's Miller Street?" the weasel, who was always interested in treasure, asked.

"Oh yes," said Kona. "Tomorrow night. A sign for the squirrel on Miller Street. I'm positive."

"So, do you know what the sign is?" asked the weasel, his sharp little nose twitching.

"No," said Kona. "Afraid not."

"Then what good are you?" the weasel sneered. And he ran off to find another weasel who might know about a sign for a squirrel on Miller Street.

The Weasel

With a sigh of relief, Kona watched the weasel run away. Then the dog turned and hurried back to Professor Albert and home, for he had a very important task ahead of him now.

Before tomorrow night, he had to think of a *sign*.

CHAPTER FOURTEEN

A Brilliant Idea

"Top won't eat his pudding and Bottom keeps trying to climb out of the box and Sparrow has the hiccups and I'm going CRAZY!" Murray yelled as Kona and Gwendolyn came into the basement that evening. "I want a night off!"

Gwendolyn clicked her claws in sympathy.

"Oh yes. Being a young mother can be so difficult at times."

A Brilliant Idea

"It sure can," agreed Murray. "And what I need is— Wait a minute! I'm not a young mother! I'm a bat!"

Gwendolyn laughed.

"Of course you are, dear."

"Well," said Murray, "truth is, I think these kids believe I *am* their mother. I mean, I'm always the one who's got the pudding. I'm always the one who rides horsey. I'm always the one going CRAZY!" The bat threw up his wings in exasperation.

"Well, tonight I hope you're the one who gets an idea," said Kona, settling Gwendolyn on top of a plastic Santa.

A Brilliant Idea

"An idea?" said Gwendolyn and Murray together.

And Kona told them about his conversation with the weasel in the park.

"The news about the sign on Miller Street will be all over town by morning," said Kona, "once that weasel starts passing it around. And Stumpy, wherever she is, is bound to hear it. I know she'll come to Miller Street tomorrow night. So we have to give her a sign, a sign that tells her this is Professor Albert's house. That we're *here*. It's our only chance, because goodness knows we'll never find *her*."

"Let's think aloud," said Gwendolyn, ever ready to get down to business. "Now, what do we know about little Stumpy that might give us some idea for a sign?"

"She's a mother," said Kona.

"She likes egg rolls," said Murray.

"She doesn't understand what a television is," said Kona.

"She collects things," said Murray.

"The collection!" said Gwendolyn. "Kona dear, is there anything from her collection we could use to signal her to this house?"

A Brilliant Idea

Kona thought of the terrible sight of the shattered pin oak in Gooseberry Park. The crews with chain saws. The remains of the cozy nest.

"No," he said sadly. "I don't think there is anything at all left of Stumpy's collection. I didn't see a single ice-cream stick or gum wrapper when I went back with Professor Albert. Besides, how would she see such a small thing at night?"

"She will be so upset," continued Kona, "losing all her treasure. Even more upset than when she lost that wonderful watch."

"What watch?" asked Murray.

"A glow-in-the-dark watch Stumpy found on a picnic table," explained Kona. "She loved it. But somebody stole it."

"Wow, it really glowed in the dark?" asked the bat.

"Yes, it—"

"That's it!" cried Gwendolyn.

"What?" Kona and Murray jumped at the same time.

"We have to find that watch," answered the crab.

A Brilliant Idea

"The watch that glows. The watch that glows *in the dark*. If we put it on the roof, Stumpy will see it glowing. And she'll know it's the sign!"

"But, Gwendolyn," said Kona, "how will we ever find that watch? Stumpy searched and searched and she never found it. We haven't a clue. We haven't a lead. We haven't a—"

"Weasel," finished Gwendolyn.

"A what?" asked Kona.

"We haven't a weasel," said the crab, "and we need one. As you discovered, dear, the weasels know everything. Find a weasel and you'll find the watch. Find the watch and you'll find Stumpy."

"Find me a hamburger," said Murray, "and I'll find fries."

Kona smiled thankfully at Gwendolyn. A good friend was good to have. But an old and *wise* friend was even better.

Things were looking up.

CHAPTER FIFTEEN

Yet Another Muckraker

There are muckrakers everywhere, mucking about in everyone's business, and Gooseberry Park certainly had its fair share. Especially on the West Side. It didn't take Kona long to find another weasel. And this time Kona had an advantage: this time Kona had *Murray*.

As Professor Albert and Kona walked toward the park the following morning, the little silver-and-black bat zipped around in the sky, just above their heads. Occasionally the bat faked a dive-bomb straight for the big dog's nose, which caused Kona to leap and Professor Albert to shriek.

"What *is* that bat doing, Kona?" Professor Albert cried, waving his arms wildly at the little figure in the sky.

Kona knew exactly what that bat was doing and he knew exactly what a good dog should do in such a case—though he really wasn't in the mood. But he stood tall and barked and barked and barked. Professor Albert was very proud. Murray was hysterical.

However, the mischievous bat did keep a low profile for the rest of the walk. Then once Professor Albert was settled and reading (this time it was snails), Murray flew down to join Kona, who was heading for the West Side.

"Very funny, Murray," said Kona as he raced across the park.

"You thought so, too?" called the bat from the air. "Oh, I was dying! Dying!"

Kona gave a huff of disapproval and ran on.

Yet Another Muckraker

When they reached the infamous west side of Gooseberry Park, Murray did an *Oh-that's-just-awful* routine, and sure enough, a weasel popped up out of nowhere.

"Something going on?" he said in a low voice.

"There certainly is, if you must know," answered the little bat, perching on a bush near Kona's head. "This dog here says he knows the identity of a thief, a thief who stole a very valuable piece of jewelry from a friend of mine. And do you know that this dog wants me to *pay* him for the name of the thief? Now, is that awful or what?"

The weasel narrowed his weasely eyes (a common response among weasels) and said to Kona, "That so?"

"A dog's got to make a living," said Kona. The weasel nodded, looking shrewdly at the dog.

"What makes you think you know who the thief is?" the weasel asked Kona.

"None of your business," said the dog.

"What's the piece of jewelry anyway?" asked the weasel.

"None of your business again," said the dog.

"It's a glow-in-the-dark watch!" said Murray.

The weasel's eyes lit up. At once Kona could see that the weasel knew who had the watch! (Kona finally believed it: weasels knew *everything*.) Now all Kona and Murray had to do was bait him.

"What's the dog's price?" the weasel hissed toward Murray.

"Egg rolls," answered the bat.

"Egg rolls?" repeated the weasel. "How many egg rolls?"

"Six of 'em, can you believe it?" answered the bat. "I told him only three, but *no-o-o-o*, he wants six. No wonder he's so fat."

The little bat grinned as Kona gave him a sharp look.

"Six, huh?" said the weasel, thinking things over. He moved closer to where the bat perched and said quietly, "Suppose I give you the information you want and you give me five egg rolls?"

"Five?" cried the bat. "Highway robbery!"

The weasel smiled.

Yet Another Muckraker

"You won't get the information anywhere else for less," he said.

"Oh yeah? Just watch me!" The little bat lifted to fly away.

"Three!" shouted the weasel. "Three egg rolls." The thought had him drooling.

Murray perched again.

"Two," he said. "I bring two, and you tell me who's got the watch."

The weasel knew Murray had him. Any weasel in the park would probably sell the name for just one egg roll. Weasels had no scruples. And they were all so sick of eating mice.

"Deal!" hissed the weasel.

"Deal!" shouted Murray, and off he flew to the Chinese Dumpster. Kona, pretending to be angry at losing six egg rolls, glared at the weasel and trotted away (actually, back to the South Side, where he would wait for Murray's return).

The old professor had fallen asleep (snails can be so tedious) by the time Murray finally came barreling back to Kona through the trees. Murray landed on the professor's head.

Yet Another Muckraker

"Murray!" Kona jumped up. "Be careful!"

"Don't worry," said the bat. "I have very delicate little feet. He can't feel a thing."

"Who has the watch?" Kona asked.

"First let me say that if I ever see another weasel again it will be too soon."

"Who has it?"

"I'm ashamed to tell you," said the bat, dropping his head.

"Who?" said Kona.

"It's a disgrace," said the bat.

"*Who?*" said Kona.

"And I want you to know that every family has its black sheep," said the bat. "And I'm not it."

"*WHO, Murray, WHO?*" cried the dog.

"My big fat cousin Ralph," answered the bat.

"What? Your cousin?" Kona asked. "Your *cousin* stole Stumpy's watch?"

"Ralph the Mouth, we call him. Eats *all* the time. If you think I'm bad, you should meet Ralph."

"But why did he steal Stumpy's watch?" asked Kona.

"Oh, it's so tacky. *Tacky!*" said Murray.

"Why?"

"The light attracts moths," Murray answered. "Ralph—who lives on the roof of Malley's Department Store, by the way—Ralph just sits there on the roof with the watch glowing every night and his mouth wide open. Isn't that disgusting? I can't understand who'd want a moth anyway, with all the Dumpsters in the world. Why, I've found whole pepperoni pizzas. Chicken nuggets. French toast with syrup!"

"Murray," said Kona impatiently, "forget Ralph's bad taste. You have to get that watch."

Murray sighed.

"Boy, is my aunt Olive going to be mad at me."

"Aunt Olive?"

"Ralph's mother. She'll never speak to me again if I take that watch. She probably thinks he won it in a poker game."

"I'll never speak to you again if you *don't* take it," said Kona.

"No more Thanksgiving dinners at Aunt Olive's house," said Murray, shaking his head sadly.

"You have to," Kona said sternly.

"No more beet casseroles."

"You have to do it, Murray."

"No more mashed turnips."

"Murray, I'm not kidding."

"No more fried liver— Hey, wait a minute! I *hate* all that stuff! Yuck! Ack! Yes, oh *yes,* I'll get that watch. I will *love* getting that watch! Just watch me!

Ha, ha, get it?" Murray danced on Professor Albert's head. The old professor mumbled and shifted.

"Hurry, Murray," Kona urged. "We need that watch by tonight. Stumpy will be running through the trees on Miller Street all evening, I'm sure of it. We need that watch."

"You've got it," said Murray. "By supper time. By the way, is this lasagna night?"

"Hurry!" Kona implored.

"I'm off," the little bat said, leaping from the professor's head. "Save me some garlic bread, Kona!"

Away the bat flew, a tiny speck in the sky. Kona watched him until he was out of sight.

"We've almost found you, Stump," the good dog whispered. "Almost."

CHAPTER SIXTEEN

The Sign

Murray arrived with the watch still in time for lasagna. He zipped down the chimney, popped out into the living room, and plunked the precious object at the feet of Kona, who was sleeping beneath Gwendolyn's bowl. Professor Albert had gone out to play bingo.

"Wonderful job, dear!" Gwendolyn applauded with her claws.

Kona jumped to his feet at the sound of her voice.

"It's here? We have it?" he asked.

The Sign

"Ta-da!" Murray pointed to the watch on the floor.

The dog took one look and nearly burst into tears. But he knew that would be a very undoglike thing to do.

"Murray," Kona said, "after dinner you'll have to take the watch up to the roof and stay there for the rest of the night. Until Stumpy finds you."

"Right-o," said Murray. "I could use some fresh air anyway. You wouldn't believe my cousin Ralph's apartment. All those pieces of moth. Yuck."

"Did you have any trouble, dear?" asked Gwendolyn.

"Nah," said Murray. "Ralph was napping—his *second* favorite hobby. Besides, I've been sneaking things out of places all my life."

"If Stumpy shows up tonight, you'll have more sneaking to do," said Kona. "Sneaking her *in.*"

"A snap," said Murray. "This house is full of holes."

"Wake me up, dear, if I'm sleeping," said Gwendolyn.

The Sign

"Me, too," said Kona.

"I'll never understand animals who sleep at night," Murray said, shaking his head. "They miss all the good stuff."

After he gobbled down a huge plate of lasagna and garlic bread, the little bat picked up the watch and flew out to the roof to wait for Stumpy.

Inside the house the night seemed endless. The professor came back home and went to bed. Kona and Gwendolyn went down and tended to the sleeping babies awhile, then returned upstairs. They were restless, constantly listening for footsteps on the roof, forever looking out the window.

"What time is it, dear?" Gwendolyn asked.

"The news is over; Professor Albert's in bed. It must be past midnight."

"Poor little Stumpy," said Gwendolyn. "All alone out there, worried so for her children. Natural disasters are hard on families."

"Especially families that live in trees," added Kona.

The old crab nodded.

The Sign

The two friends talked and talked and waited and waited.

Up on the roof Murray was keeping himself occupied by making lists in his head. First he listed things that were green: limes, olives, Christmas trees, Kermit the Frog. He listed yellow things: corn, sunflowers, lemons, Big Bird. Blue things: swimming pools, berries, the sky, Cookie Monster. (Murray had watched a lot of *Sesame Street* in Professor Albert's house.) He had gone through a purple list, an orange list, a red list, and a white list, and was just beginning a striped list when he heard someone in the trees whisper his name.

"Murray?"

The little bat jumped. For a second he forgot about Stumpy and thought his cousin Ralph had found him.

"Nope!" he said.

"Murray, it *is* you!" A little shadow with a big fluffy tail leaped from way up in the trees and landed on the roof with a thump. Murray knew that tail.

The Sign

"Stumpy! Stumpy!" He jumped up and down, flapping his wings. "Good golly, Miss Molly!"

The little red squirrel scurried across the roof and into the light of the watch. Tears were streaming down her face, which made tears stream down Murray's face, and the two stood there on the roof together, hugging and crying.

"My babies?" sobbed Stumpy.

"Fat and sassy!" sobbed Murray.

"Kona?" the little squirrel cried.

"Fat and bossy!" Murray cried harder.

The Sign

Stumpy laughed and began to wipe away Murray's tears.

"And you, Murray?" she asked gently.

"Just *fat!*" answered the little bat with a teary grin. "And I bet I have the *worst* garlic breath."

Murray sneaked Stumpy through a crack in the house's foundation, and the little mother ran straight across the basement to where her babies lay sleeping. She jumped into the box and picked up all three at once, holding them tight and kissing their little red heads. The children were drowsy, half-asleep. But they seemed to recognize their lost mother, for they held tight to her with their tiny paws. Murray thought he might start bawling again.

The Sign

"Where are Kona and Gwendolyn?" Stumpy asked over her children's sleeping heads.

"I forgot!" cried Murray. "I was supposed to tell them first thing!"

Murray flew up the basement steps and did a snappy tap dance across the living room floor.

Kona raised his big head. He looked at Murray.

"Is she here?" Kona asked anxiously.

With a big grin, Murray nodded excitedly and pointed toward the basement.

"Stump!" Kona called. He picked up Gwendolyn—whose antennae flew at the sound of Stumpy's name—and everyone ran for the basement.

The joy the friends shared in their reunion was the best treasure of all to be found on Miller Street that evening. And Kona surprised himself.

He cried.

CHAPTER SEVENTEEN

The Wonders of Technology

Life in Professor Albert's house for the next several days was magical.

Stumpy's wanderings had left her rather thin, so Kona took on the job of fattening her up. Food upstairs continued to disappear at a steady pace. Poor Professor Albert was making trips to the grocery daily. He had decided a sneaky chipmunk definitely was stealing the food, and he contrived several schemes for hiding his groceries. None of them worked, of course. Not with an experienced bat in the house.

Kona had promised himself that once this adventure was over, he would be a perfect dog for Professor Albert forever, to repay him for all the food they'd borrowed and the lamp he'd crashed. He would never pull at the leash. He would never bark at the UPS truck. He would never drip water from his bowl onto the kitchen floor. He would be perfect.

With Murray's help, Kona sneaked boxes of shredded wheat, bags of English muffins, and jars of Spanish peanuts downstairs to his guests. Stumpy's health improved each day, and her children were very happy to have real squirrel milk to grow on again.

Stumpy had told her friends the whole story of her night in the ice storm—how she had left her children in Murray's care, believing she could find Paradise Lane and Kona. She knew Kona would give shelter to them all. But of course, Paradise Lane was the wrong road completely; it was even on the wrong side of town, and for two days Stumpy had wandered

The Wonders of Technology

through all of its yards and trees, looking for a chocolate Labrador.

Then, the third day, on the upper end of Paradise Lane, she saw from high up in a tree a yard where about twenty chocolate Labradors were playing. She thought she was dreaming! She rubbed her eyes hard and looked again. Yes, it was twenty chocolate Labradors, and they all looked like Kona!

Believing she had finally found the house of her friend, Stumpy leaped from the trees, ran across the power lines to the other side of the street, and hopped onto the gate of the yard. She wasn't sure which dog was Kona, they all looked so much alike,

The Wonders of Technology

so she stood up and yelled as loudly as she could, "KONA, I'M HERE!"

And ... BARK! BARK! BARK! BARK! BARK! BARK! BARK! Those Labradors chased her right off that gate and into a tree, and they stood under that tree barking at her all day until a woman came home and put them back in the house.

Poor Stumpy. She was very confused, for she did not understand the dogs' unfriendly behavior. They were not at all like Kona. She managed to make her way back to Gooseberry Park, then was stunned when there was no sign of Murray or the children. Her tree was gone. Her family was gone. Her friend was gone. She wandered the town, asking for news of a chocolate dog who might be looking for her. No one could help.

The Wonders of Technology

But then one day, while she still searched, word began to spread about a dog, and a sign for a squirrel on Miller Street. In the morning the rumor traveled through every den in Gooseberry Park (beginning on the West Side, of course). In the afternoon it went above ground and through every tree still standing. By supper time it was out on the street. And at nightfall, when Stumpy wearily asked an old pigeon sitting on the courthouse lawn whether he'd heard of a dog who might be looking for her, the rumor finally hit its target. The old pigeon, who knew every neighborhood in the city, led the little squirrel directly to Miller Street. And the soft green glow of the wonderful watch on the roof of Professor Albert's house led her to Kona.

After staying in the professor's basement for a few days, Stumpy became curious about the way people in houses live. So when Professor Albert was away, Kona would accompany her about the rooms and show her all the wonders of technology she had missed by living in trees.

The Wonders of Technology

Kona showed her the professor's clock radio, his compact disc player, his electric can opener, his VCR with remote control, his toaster, his heating pad, and his refrigerator.

Stumpy was very impressed by all of the food Professor Albert had stored in his refrigerator. Staring at the shelves, she said, "He must have collected all summer long to get this much food put away."

"Oh no," said Kona. "He got most of it just this week."

"Amazing!" Stumpy exclaimed.

But of all Professor Albert's technological wonders, it was his television that Stumpy liked best of all. When her children were asleep and the professor was out, Stumpy would sneak upstairs to see what was on. Because she had always been a very practical squirrel, she liked the PBS station best. She listened to every word of *Wall Street Week* and *The Frugal Gourmet.* But *This Old House* was her favorite, and once, when Professor Albert and Kona were off for a walk, she crept upstairs into the kitchen and fixed the professor's leaky faucet.

It was all quite extraordinary.

The Wonders of Technology

CHAPTER EIGHTEEN

A New Home

After a week or so had passed and Stumpy was strong and healthy enough to be on her own, the friends began talking about finding a new tree for Stumpy and Murray to live in. The two had become like family—especially since Stumpy's children were forever forgetting and calling Murray "Mama"—and it seemed only logical the two should do their house-hunting together.

But Kona, always protective, suggested instead that he do the hunting. Now that the weather was so pleasant, he and Professor Albert were taking

A New Home

walks to the park every day, sometimes two or three times. And Kona had made so many acquaintances in Gooseberry Park since the evening of Stumpy's disappearance that he was sure he could find some-one to help him scout things out.

Gwendolyn agreed with the plan.

"Moving makes children nervous," she told Stumpy confidentially. "It's best that Kona find some-thing for you that's all ready and waiting. Then you and the babies can move right in, without too much confusion."

"You're very wise, Gwendolyn," Stumpy told the crab.

"Well . . ." The crab smiled. "One of the benefits of age."

A remarkable fact of nature is that problems al-most always get solved just when they are meant to. And those who can help solve the problems almost always show up at just the right time.

Thus it seemed completely logical that as soon as Kona went looking for someone who might help him locate a new house for his friends, he ran into

A New Home

Conroy, the famous cat. Kona did not know it yet, but running into Conroy was a stroke of good fortune.

"Hey, it's the skating dog," the cat said with a grin, scratching his back against a knobby tree stump.

Kona blushed with embarrassment.

"No, it's cool," assured the cat. "Word of your heroics got around. Even I was impressed."

"Thank you," Kona said gladly.

"So, what's happening?" asked the cat.

And Kona explained what he was searching for.

"You need a tip on a good piece of real estate?" Conroy asked.

Kona nodded.

"You found the right man, my friend." The cat rolled onto his back. "I heard about a place just yesterday," he continued, scratching his back against the grass. "Nice little joint. South Side. Some starlings moved out and went to Florida because of Granny's arthritis."

"How do you know?" asked Kona.

A New Home

"They were always pecking at my head," Conroy answered. "Lovely family," he said sarcastically. "Just hated to see 'em go! You'd better hustle, though. Good trees are scarce since the storm. It won't stay empty for long."

"Gosh," said Kona, turning to go. "I've got to get my friends in there. Today!"

The dog started running.

"Thanks, Conroy!" he called back.

The cat took a deep bow and strolled on.

Kona practically dragged Professor Albert all the

A New Home

way home. *After today,* thought Kona. *After today, I'll be perfect.*

The professor kept muttering something about how he should have bought a guinea pig instead of a Labrador. But Kona knew he didn't mean it.

Once they were home, Kona sneaked down to the basement and told Stumpy and Murray the time had come. It was moving day.

"Really?" Stumpy asked.

"Does that mean I'll miss pork chop night?" asked Murray.

Within minutes they were set to go.

"Murray," said Kona, "Stumpy and the kids will ride on my back."

"Right," said the bat, hopping around and testing his wings.

"And you have to fly," said Kona.

"Gee," the bat said, looking at Kona in exasperation, "thanks for helping me figure that out."

"But first you have to be bait," said Kona.

"Excuse me?" said Murray. "Don't you mean *bat?*"

A New Home

"No. *Bait.* You have to go upstairs and flap around the living room," Kona explained, "to make Professor Albert open all the doors and windows. Then you have to get him to chase you into the bedroom so I can get us out the front door."

The bat grinned. "This sounds like fun!"

"Just don't get clobbered," Kona said.

"No problem!"

The dog, with the squirrels on his back, stood ready at the bottom of the steps.

"OK, Murray—GO!" he yelled.

The little bat saluted and went flapping wildly up the steps and into the living room. The next thing everyone heard was Professor Albert screaming and flinging all the doors and windows open. Then they heard him grab the colander off the kitchen wall and run madly toward the bedroom.

"Let's go!" cried Kona. He raced up the steps and straight out the front door. As they were leaving,

A New Home

Stumpy and the babies waved cheerfully to Gwendolyn, who from her bowl hailed them with a claw.

Kona galloped down the sidewalk as the squirrels hung on and cheered. He loved being a hero again.

They made it to the south side of Gooseberry Park, then after a few queries they found the tree where the starlings had been living. Except for a few sunflower seed hulls and a half-eaten hot dog bun, the place was empty. And, like Conroy had promised, it was a dream.

"It's a split-level!" Stumpy called down to Kona in delight. "Murray can take the upper and we can take the lower! And it's in a sugar maple! Just like the one I was born in!"

A New Home

Kona looked up and smiled. He waited while Stumpy and her children wandered the rooms. Stumpy poked her head out of a hole.

"And there's plenty of room for treasure!" she called.

Kona sighed with pleasure.

While the dog was imagining all the new treasure Stumpy would be collecting, suddenly Murray came careening through the trees. He grabbed on to a

A New Home

branch of the maple, whirled and bounced, then hung there, bobbing like a spring.

"Wow!" he cried.

"Are you all right?" Kona called.

"I'm all right," said the little bat, brushing himself off. "But it's sure too bad about that television!"

CHAPTER NINETEEN

The Wonderful Watch

By the middle of the summer, Professor Albert had replaced the thirty-inch television he had cracked with a flying colander, and Kona had taught Bottom to catch a tiny Frisbee in his mouth. Sparrow and Top had their mother's interests: they collected things, and they spent hours down on the riverbank seeing what people might have thrown out that day. Stumpy spent her time as usual: housekeeping

The Wonderful Watch

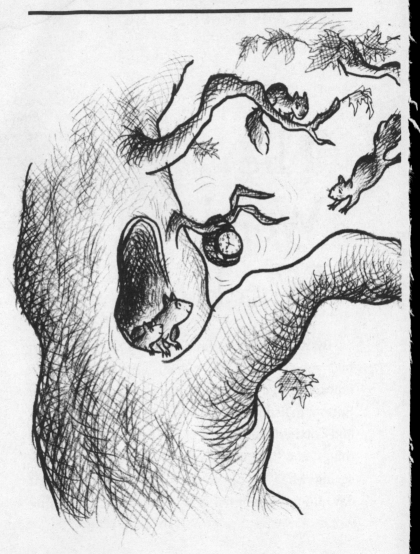

The Wonderful Watch

(well, a little); food collecting (she didn't trust Murray's hand-to-mouth existence); and admiring all the new treasures her children were bringing home.

Beside the front door of Stumpy and Murray's dear home hung the wonderful and famous glow-in-the-dark watch. It cast its green heavenly light all around, and this time every animal in the park seemed respectful of the halo. Even Ralph.

When Stumpy's children were old enough to stay out at night with friends, Stumpy would point to a number on the watch's face.

"Be home by this time," she would say like a good mother. And the children were.

And though Murray continued to bump his way through Gooseberry Park on his forays out for egg rolls or curly fries, he never ever bumped into his own tree again. From wherever he was, the glow of the watch led him safely back.

And across the way, on Miller Street, in Professor Albert's peaceful house . . .

The Wonderful Watch

Late at night Kona and Gwendolyn would sit together and talk of all the wonderful adventures they had had. They loved retelling their favorite Murray stories. They loved chatting about the children. And from time to time, Kona had to recount yet again his magnificent journey across the ice.

The two old friends would talk through the deep night, and now and then they would look over to the window, across the tops of the houses, and up into the familiar trees. There, in the darkness, they could see a lovely green radiance, a welcoming light . . . a treasure in Gooseberry Park.

The devils' coach

The
devils' coach

JIM BROCK
and
Joe Gilmartin

David C. Cook Publishing Co.
ELGIN, ILLINOIS—WESTON, ONTARIO
FULLERTON, CALIFORNIA

Published by David C. Cook Publishing Co., Elgin, IL 60120
Edited by Ronald Wilson and Marshall Shelley
Cover illustration by Vaccaro Associates, Inc. Gabriel Hoyes, artist
Cover and photo section design by Wendell Mathews
Printed in the United States of America

Library of Congress Catalog Number 77-87255
ISBN 0-89191-103-0

To my wife, also my best friend, who prayed that I would stay in coaching until I found out why I was there; and to my sister, clearly one of the saints, who persisted in Christian love until I learned what that meant.

CONTENTS

Winning Is . . .

1

AN OLD GREEK PROVERB says that when the gods
are truly angry with a man, they give him what he
wants. I don't know what I did to those gods, but
whatever it was must have made them absolutely
furious. They seemed to give me almost everything I
wanted.

But somehow, the more they gave, the less satisfied I became. Success as a coach almost drove me
out of baseball. I had always believed that winning
is everything. Yet, after winning almost everything,
something was still definitely missing.

Whatever it was wasn't obvious to anyone else, but
I felt it. And my wife Pat felt it more than I did.

The search for whatever-it-was had a rather hum-
ble beginning. I was one of those fortunate people
who always knew what he wanted to become. Ever
since I was a sophomore in high school, I knew what
I wanted to do.

My dad thought he knew, too. He was sure I was

11

going to be a big-league pitcher. Although he never specifically mentioned the Hall of Fame, there was probably no doubt in his mind that his son would someday be enshrined there.

My dad was a tremendous man, but about as poor a judge of baseball talent as you could imagine. He wasn't even close.

In high school I realized I couldn't play that well, but it didn't really matter, because I knew I wanted to coach. In fact, I remember doing a little coaching on the high school team—not that my coach ever asked for my advice.

I continued to play as a strictly mediocre pitcher throughout high school and the first two years of college. All I wanted was to keep playing so that when a break came my way, I'd know enough to coach.

During the summer after my senior year in high school, when I was barely eighteen years old, I coached (officially) for the first time—an American Legion Class B team. The next summer, I coached a Class A team, and the summer after that we won the state and regional titles. My career was off and running.

Eventually our team, Kerr Sporting Goods of Phoenix, won the American Legion World Championship. I remember thinking that Vince Lombardi and John Wooden didn't win anything big until after they were fifty. Here I was at twenty-five and already had a world championship. But I wasn't satisfied.

I started asking myself what it would take to make

me a happy person. I decided that the answer was to get a job as head coach of some major high school in the Phoenix area. That should do it.

Well, it wasn't very long after I put my wish into words that Mesa High School offered me that baseball job, and I thought, this is it. This is where I've always wanted to be.

Pitching against us in my first game as coach was a kid named Jim Palmer. Even then, it was obvious he was a great athlete. He was about 6' 5", and we repeated jokes about how he had callouses on the backs of his hands because his arms were so long they dragged the ground.

Palmer didn't have very good control, or much of an idea of what he was doing out there, but he probably threw harder then than he does now in the majors. Because his arm was so long and loose, he got tremendous rotation on the ball, and it just exploded. His fastball was more alive than any high-school pitcher's I'd ever seen. It was unbelievable.

We'd heard about Palmer, of course, so we prepared for him. We got a pitching machine and moved it in to thirty feet so we could get around on the fastball.

But during the game, we discovered that Palmer's ball was so alive and moved so much that timing was just part of the problem.

Fortunately, our pitcher was throwing a great game, too, and going into the bottom of the last inning, the score was 0-0. With two outs, up to the plate walked big Jim Palmer.

13

Since we were playing on a wide-open field with no fence, I moved our centerfielder back until I could barely see him. I knew a single, a double, or a triple wouldn't hurt us. The thing we had to guard against was the home run.

Palmer didn't hit the ball often, but when he did, it was unreal. Unfortunately, this was one of those times.

When he hit the ball, at first I thought it was a pop-up. He hit it extremely high, but it kept going. My centerfielder started back . . . and ran, and ran, and ran. And he didn't come close to it.

We lost 1-0 on a 500-foot pop-up.

Somehow, after that loss, high-school coaching didn't really seem like all that much happiness. It was what I'd wanted. But now that I was there, it didn't seem to be such a big deal.

A couple years later, I was asked to start a baseball program at Mesa Community College. I thought surely this must be it. Junior college was as high as I'd ever played, so it would certainly be as high as I'd ever coach. I waited for happiness to fall on me, but, strangely, the thrill of being a juco coach didn't seem to do it.

I remember my first game at the college. It didn't last long for me, thanks to a man named Stan Landis. Stan was a major-league umpire who was really slumming when he worked junior-college games. He did it to pick up some extra money and to tune up for the major-league season a few months away. (Our season started in February.)

Since this was the season opener, I was keyed up, and so were all the players. In the third inning there was a close play at home. Stan was about twenty feet from the plate, didn't even bend over, and seemed to be totally disinterested as he called our runner out.

I wasn't sure if he was out or safe, but I couldn't believe an umpire could be so nonchalant about a call. I promptly told him so. Apparently Stan didn't think any JC coach anywhere would question a big-league umpire. (I never had very good sense anyway.) He told me that if I opened my mouth again the rest of the game, he would throw me out. I decided not to say any more then, and I retreated to the dugout.

At the old Mesa Rendezvous Park, each dugout was extended by a chalk-lined area where bats, helmets, and chairs were kept. Before the game, while going over the ground rules, we'd decided that those areas were part of the dugout. So that's where I stood.

Stan looked over and yelled at me to get back into the dugout.

I said, "If you'd pay more attention to the calls at home instead of where I'm standing, you'd probably be a better umpire."

Shortly after that, I got to see the next six innings of my first game as a college coach from the stands.

Junior college didn't seem to be that much different from American Legion or high-school coaching. Since simply being a junior college coach didn't satisfy me, I decided what I needed was to be able to say I was a *good* juco coach. That should do it.

The first three seasons at Mesa were building years. But in 1969, everything seemed to jell. We finished the season with a 21-10 record by relying mostly on our offensive output—a .312 team batting average and sixty-six stolen bases. We won the conference, the district—and suddenly, we were on our way to Grand Junction, Colorado, for the national championship tournament.

I had only one dependable starting pitcher that year. His name was Don Formiller. Any time a team plays in a tournament and has six games in six days, a coach has to scramble for pitching. In my case, it was worse than scrambling—it was Formiller and pray for rain.

Panola Junior College from Carthage, Texas, beat us in the second round to dump us into the losers' bracket, but we kept scratching and clawing, desperately trying to keep from being eliminated.

Three games and three victories later, we found ourselves playing for the national championship against—you guessed it—the Panola Ponies.

I had to throw Formiller, even though he'd had only one day of rest. Pitching for Panola was Doug Ault, a lefthander with a jug-handle curve who had handcuffed us in the second game. The stage was set for the showdown. It should have been a terrific pitching duel.

It wasn't.

Both teams scored a run in the first inning. Then Formiller and Ault settled down to pitch scoreless baseball for the next three.

16

In the bottom of the fourth, Formiller started to weaken. He gave up a single and two walks to load the bases with no outs. I knew it was time for a change, so I brought in Dale Goodman. Dale got the first batter out. That brought up Panola's shortstop. He swung at one of Goodman's pitches, and his bat ticked our catcher's glove. The umpire called interference, bringing home one run.

That seemed to unleash the Ponies. They hit a bases-loaded double to knock in three more runs and a two-run, 345-foot homer to cap the inning.

Down 7-1, we knew we'd have to come back tough.

During our turn to bat the next inning, Goodman must have been smarting from the pounding he'd just taken, because he beat out an infield hit. Two walks loaded the bases, and suddenly we were threatening.

Ken Reed, our second baseman, bounced to third. The Pony third baseman threw to the plate. The ball reached the catcher a split second before Goodman did. But Dale hit him low, and as the catcher crashed to the ground, the ball popped loose, and everyone was safe.

With the bases still loaded, Ault walked our right-fielder Roger Schmuck to force in a run. Then Phil Vetter stroked a double off the right-centerfield wall to score two more. We had runners on second and third, with one out, trailing 7-5.

Our next batter tapped a bouncer to second base, and again Panola tried to cut off the run at the plate. Schmuck barreled into the Pony catcher and jarred

17

the ball loose. After that, Ault retired the side, but we'd moved to within one, 7-6.

Panola managed another run in the bottom of the fifth, and we had to bear down a bit harder to catch up.

Somehow, the hits just weren't there. Ault was relieved in the seventh inning by Hardy Frazier, who held us hitless the final three innings.

We had run out of pitching, out of hits, out of steam, out of everything. It was over, 8-6.

We left the next day on our long drive back home. We'd lost the championship, and I wasn't happy. But I could see now what happiness was—the junior college national championship.

Happiness was two more runs.

Thirty-Second Thrills

2

WE HAD OUR CHANCE FOR REVENGE the next year. The 1970 version of the Mesa HoKams won the conference, the district, and the right to go to Grand Junction again for the National Junior College Athletic Association baseball tournament. Happiness was almost at hand.

The first round pitted us against our enemies from the year before, the Panola Ponies.

We'd found out that the previous year, just before the championship game, Panola coach Bill Griffin had sent each of his players a powder puff wrapped in a nice box with a note: "This is what we think of you. Signed: Jim Brock."

It was corny and old-fashioned—but it had worked. After the final game the Panola players came up to our guys and said, "So you think we're powder puffs, huh?" Only then did we all find out what Griffin had pulled.

In 1970 we were out to avenge both the prank and our defeat. That first-round shootout was a wild one. Doug Ault was on the mound again for Panola. We countered with our ace, Jimmy Otten. In the bottom of the ninth, we were behind by two runs. We scratched out a single, got a walk, and then a clutch double by our little center fielder Dennis Kendrick tied up the game 5-5.

Three extra innings went scoreless. Then in the top of the thirteenth, Panola pushed three runs across the plate. It looked like we were done for.

But in the bottom of the inning, Ault finally lost his control. He walked three men and hit a fourth with a pitch, which forced across one run. Coach Griffin brought in a reliever.

With the bases still loaded, our third baseman Kim Short punched a single, scoring two runs and tying the game 8-8. I sent in a pinch hitter, Herb Genung, to hit for our pitcher. Genung made me look good by blooping a fly ball that dropped into left field. One run scored, the game was over, and we had beaten Panola 9-8.

The rest of the tournament was almost anticlimactic. We lost a game to Columbia, Georgia, but came back through the losers' bracket and beat Mesa College of Colorado 8-0 for the championship.

We'd made it! What excitement! What a thrill! People swarmed us on the field. After five years at Mesa, I'd coached a national championship team.

People continued to congratulate me . . . for about two weeks. Then a funny thing happened. The compliments stopped. The fans wanted to know about next year. I'd won the national championship, but nothing had really changed. I still had the same doubts and frustrations with coaching that I'd had before. That elusive feeling of satisfaction had slipped away sometime during those few weeks.

Then somebody told me that no one had ever won two junior college championships in a row. I thought, well, maybe that was the answer—to accomplish something nobody else had ever done. That had to be the ticket to happiness.

Our prospects were pretty solid at the beginning of 1971, but it turned out to be one of the longest seasons of my life. We had injury problems, disciplinary problems, academic problems, coaching problems. It seemed like the whole season would collapse any time.

Half a dozen times I thought we would be eliminated from contention, but somehow we'd get a run or two in the ninth and hang on. Almost miraculously, we made it back to Grand Junction.

In almost identical fashion to previous years, we were beaten in the second round and had to come back through the losers' bracket. But again we made it to the final game, this time against Miami Dade North Junior College from Florida.

Finally, there was a fly ball hit to the outfield, our center fielder squeezed it for the final out, our fans streamed onto the field, and bedlam broke loose. For the first time ever, a school won the national championship two years in a row.

My assistant coach was almost hysterical. He was jumping around yelling, "We did it, coach, we did it!"

Then he looked at me and suddenly stopped.

"What's wrong, coach?" he asked.

"I'm really tired," I told him. "And if we don't get home early enough tomorrow to start recruiting, there's no way we can win this title again next year."

Tired? Was that the only feeling I could manage after a victory like that? If the agony of defeat is supposed to last forever, shouldn't the thrill of victory last more than thirty seconds?

A New
Head Devil

3

IT TAKES FOURTEEN HOURS to drive from Grand Junction, Colorado, to Mesa, Arizona. During that trip, instead of happily reliving each of the victories, I did more soul searching than I'd ever done in my whole life.

My team had made it to three straight national championship finals and had won an unprecedented two straight national titles. I'd been named the national junior college coach of the year twice.

The goal I just had to reach, the thing I would have sacrificed anything for, I had achieved last night. But the thrill slid out the window almost as fast as it arrived.

It was a momentary high—very momentary. I thought that drugs and drinking were also momentary highs—people trying to turn on for thirty seconds to forget how unhappy they are. During that fourteen-hour trip, I realized that it could happen in coaching, too.

I admitted to myself that I wasn't happy. I was neither a good husband nor a good father—not even much of a person. My wife, I realized, had become an expert at hiding the kids after daddy lost, even hiding the dog. At times, my kids were afraid of me.

Two or three days before any big ball game, the pressure would get to me, and I'd quit talking to anybody. My family and my players both suffered. Not only had I become a demanding coach but a terribly intimidating one as well.

My coaching philosophy was simple: If my team won, my job was just to stay out of the way, because the players would celebrate anyway. If they lost, my job was to make it such a miserable experience they would never want to do that again. If we won, it was because I was a great coach; if we lost, it was because the players were a bunch of turkeys. It wasn't a pleasant philosophy, but it appeared to work.

I had set goals for myself, and I had reached them. But, strangely, when I got there, I found nothing.

During this musing, I came to the conclusion that I hated coaching. Obviously, I had a vocational problem. I was in the wrong job. I should get away from this miserable life of joyless victories and anger-filled defeats. I decided to go back to school, get one more degree, then get a job as a principal or athletic director ... anything where there wasn't the pressure of competition.

A funny thing happened to me on the way to that

degree. Bobby Winkles, the coach at Arizona State University, left for a job with the California Angels. Suddenly, seven miles down the road from where I was working, the best college baseball job in the country was open.

Never mind the fact that the job I had now was eating me alive. If I was anything, I was a competitive person. Who can deny what he is? This was the best job, and I had to have it.

So my wife and I conducted a whirlwind political campaign. Pat wrote scores of letters, and I called everyone I could think of, asking people to put in a good word for me with the new athletic director, Dr. Fred Miller.

Finally, after a month of hustling, Dr. Fred called and said, "Jim, it's yours."

This had to be it. I felt I was at the top of my field.

I held a press conference. (Good grief! I'd never even been to a press conference before.) Someone told me not to try any jokes because Winkles had been very funny. But I told a joke anyway, and everybody laughed. This is going to be great, I thought, and Pat and I went out that night to celebrate.

About five-thirty the next morning I woke up in a cold sweat and realized what I had done. I'd simply taken all the pressure I couldn't handle at Mesa Community College and very cleverly magnified it a thousand times. I actually gave some thought to calling another press conference and getting rid of the silly job. But even in my cold sweat, that seemed pretty tacky.

To understand how a coach with a 163-80 record can find true misery, and to appreciate the forces that were pushing me closer to the edge of a world that seemed to be getting flatter by the minute, it's necessary to understand the status of baseball at Arizona State University and the legend of Bobby Winkles.

Baseball is bigger at ASU than at perhaps any other major school—even practically perennial NCAA champion University of Southern California. The Sun Devils play their home games in an ideal campus facility, eight-thousand-seat Packard Stadium, average three thousand fans a game, and are regularly at or near the top of the NCAA attendance tree. Games with archrival University of Arizona and the NCAA playoff games regularly fill Packard to overflow. Media coverage of Sun Devil baseball ranks somewhat below Sun Devil football, but it's on a par with basketball, and it reaches the saturation point during the College World Series.

On most campuses, baseball is regarded as a pleasant spring afterthought that helps give the school a "well-rounded" program. Why the obsession at Arizona State? The reason can be put in two words: Bobby Winkles.

Winkles, a longtime minor-league infielder, arrived in 1959 at a school with absolutely no baseball pedigree and proceeded to fashion a 524-173 record over the next thirteen seasons. Along the way, he won five Western Athletic Conference—Southern Division championships, four WAC championships, four

30

NCAA District 7 championships, and (as my critics reminded me for nearly five years) three NCAA championships. Winkles also sent the likes of Reggie Jackson, Rick Monday, Sal Bando, Lenny Randle, Duffy Dyer, Larry Gura, Lerrin LaGrow, and Gary Gentry to the major leagues.

In the process, he acquired a statewide image that rivaled that of ASU football coach Frank Kush. In addition, a fanatical group of followers came to believe Winkles had invented not only baseball but also hot dogs, apple pie, and probably Chevrolet, too. He was an Arizona favorite son.

It wasn't so much what he did as the way he did it—with folksy, down-home (Swifton, Arkansas) humor, a minimum of blood and sweat, and absolutely no tears. At a time when many of his colleagues were snarling at major-league scouts for stealing their players, Winkles was playing golf with them. And the scouts were directing superb replacements to ASU for the players they took from him. His particular genius with the players was the ability to tongue-lash them within an inch of their scholarships one minute and be one of the boys the next. Most coaches have to make a choice, but Winkles was somehow able to enjoy the best of both worlds. Such was his hold on public, press, and players alike that his final official act at ASU—a dismal double defeat at home at the hands of an underdog Brigham Young University team, a defeat that knocked the Devils out of the running for another national title—didn't so much as muss a single hair of the Winkles legend.

31

So, by the time the siren song of the major leagues beckoned from California, where he ultimately became manager of the Angels, a coach with the world champion Oakland A's and San Francisco Giants before returning to manage the A's, Winkles had built something of a "Cary Grant monster." (Legend has it that a disappointed female fan, meeting Cary Grant for the first time, complained that he didn't look like Cary Grant. "Nobody does," he reportedly replied.) Nobody looked like Bobby Winkles after he left ASU. Probably not even Bobby Winkles.

But stepping into a pair of size 19 triple E shoes was only a part of the problem I faced in 1972. The other part was Winkles' desire to designate his successor—preferably one of his former pupils. Although Winkles himself got over his disappointment quickly enough, his followers never quite forgave me for usurping the throne from a rightful heir. The actual usurper, of course, was Athletic Director Fred Miller, but Dr. Fred was holding a hot hand in so many other areas, it was hard to get mad at him. Drained of the passions of the time, it seems odd that my choice generated so much backstage heat. But it did.

Fred picked me in the face of adversity. His neck was out there right along with mine. Nobody was pulling for me any harder than he was, and he's always been completely supportive. Fred is so kind and softhearted that it was amazing to me that he could succeed the way he did. From the beginning, he seemed very concerned about the pressure I was under. Just prior to that at the first press conference he explained to me that Winkles definitely cast a giant shadow, but that as it got nearer to noon, it would get smaller.

Unfortunately, the shadow theory wasn't much comfort as I entered my first season as the head Sun Devil. I found myself in a heads-you-win, tails-I-lose situation.

If Arizona State won the NCAA championship, credit would be apportioned as follows: players, 56 percent; Winkles, 43 percent; Brock, 1 percent. If ASU *didn't* win, the blame would be placed on: Winkles, nothing; players, 6 percent; umpires, 3 percent; Brock, 91 percent.

It wasn't a pleasant thought.

I knew Winkles had done a great job and had left me a fine team, so I decided to stay out of the way as much as possible. I found a spot in the dugout where I couldn't be seen from the stands, and I stayed there for seventy games. We won sixty-four of those for an NCAA record, and we earned a spot in the College World Series in Omaha. Then we lost a tough 1-0 game to the University of Southern California in the final.

To tell the truth, I was a little embarrassed when my peers voted me "Coach of the Year" and presented me the Adirondack Big Stick award and a $1,000 vacation in Hawaii. I'd never done less coaching in my life.

Someone was quoted as saying that Winkles might not have had as flashy a record, but if he'd gotten to Omaha, he would have won. I don't know if that was true or not, but I believed it. On the other hand, the fans hadn't eaten me alive for losing to USC.

The second year, 1973, we really had only four experienced people. Eddie Bane, our pitching ace from the year before, was coming back, and the other pitchers looked like they might be pretty good. There was some promise, but nothing like the great talent we'd had in 1972. I moved a lot of people around, and I felt that just getting to Omaha with that kind of a team was an accomplishment. But this was my first taste of the If-you-don't-win-at-Omaha-it's-a-bad-year syndrome. Fans had been somewhat understanding the year before, but now they were saying, "If you lose at Omaha, this is not acceptable behavior." It was almost as if they felt it would be better not to go to Omaha at all than to finish second.

We finished the season with a 59-8 record. Jimmy Otten, our number-two pitcher and the one who had played for me at Mesa, pitched the opening game at Omaha against Penn State. I wanted to save Eddie Bane for the second round. We would play the winner of the Minnesota-Oklahoma game, and those were tougher teams. The strategy worked as Otten held Penn State to one run and knocked in a run himself with a double. We won 3-1.

Minnesota beat Oklahoma, but Bane handled the Gophers easily the next day with an eight-hit shutout. We advanced, 3-0.

With 10,078 fans looking on, we ran into the bad guys from last year, the Trojans of Southern California. We were tied 1-1 in the bottom of the fifth inning when our pitcher walked the bases loaded, and a USC single scored two runs. We couldn't score after that, and the 3-1 loss dropped us into the losers' bracket.

We beat Texas the next day 6-5 in the bottom of the ninth to stay alive. And when unbeaten USC fell behind Minnesota by seven runs in their game, I thought we were in good shape. A Gopher victory would leave three teams with one loss, but the Trojans rallied to beat Minnesota. We knew we'd have to beat USC twice for the title.

I had a tough decision to make. Who should I pitch? Otten had just pitched against Texas. Bane had had only two days rest.

I asked Eddie about his arm, and he said it was a little tight. He said he could pitch, although he didn't think he would have very good stuff. Bane had been drafted in the first round that spring by the Minnesota Twins, and it was really unthinkable for me to pitch him with his arm not feeling right. He was a tremendous competitor, and there was no way that he'd say his arm was sore if it wasn't. So I simply had to start someone else.

Actually, my decision was based on two factors. First, I didn't want to risk hurting Bane's arm. And second, we had to beat USC twice for the championship anyway.

I started Jim Umbarger, who had done relief pitching for us in the two previous games. USC jumped on him for two runs in the first inning and two more in the third. Doug Slocum came in to relieve and shut out the Trojans the rest of the way. But we could manage only three runs against the USC pitching, and we lost 4-3.

When I got back to Phoenix, I got the same question over and over: "Why didn't you pitch Bane?" USC had a great ball club that year, one of the best of its championship teams, but none of our fans thought for a moment that they actually might have been superior. The only thought in everybody's mind seemed to be that I had cost ASU the national title by not pitching Bane. I began to feel a little persecuted, because I saw myself as having done a humanitarian act, and yet I was being criticized for it. I'd always had a win-at-any-cost reputation (which I felt was undeserved), but I still look back on that decision without regret.

The fans, however, continued to think I had thrown the title away, and the criticism went on and on and on. I think that incident, more than any other, really planted the seeds of paranoia in me.

It also started the first serious Brock-Must-Go movement. People felt I'd had my second chance and blown it. I guess they figured that for the first year, I was just along for the ride, trying to learn everybody's first name.

It had been bad enough to learn back at Mesa Community College that victory and happiness were not necessarily synonymous. Now I was discovering that even the search for it, which used to lead at least to momentary highs, was turning sour. I didn't handle the new discovery particularly well.

I know it's hard to believe a man with two trips to the national championships could feel so badly about his job, but I reached a point where I hated to go to work and once again cast about for an exit.

If I could have somehow gotten a doctorate in five minutes, I would have taken it and gotten out of coaching. I remember telling myself, "Okay, dummy, you're stuck. The way you make your living is by coaching, but you're never going to like it. If only you could take some kind of pressure pill to relieve the anxiety, you might be all right, but there isn't any such pill, so you've got to find some way out on your own terms." To me, the doctorate was that way.

Wistfully, I thought back to the days of high-school coaching. I was close to the players in age, and everything was fun. Legion ball was even more so. I knew I couldn't scream at Legion players—they might just go home.

I can pinpoint the precise point the pressure was turned on and the fun off. It was after my third year at Mesa. The first three years had been happy ones because we had a brand new program, and nobody expected too much. But we went into that fourth year with practically everybody back from a good team, and the expectations started. That was in 1969, the first of five straight years that my teams reached national finals. By 1974 those expectations (spelled p-r-e-s-s-u-r-e) had grown to almost unmanageable proportions.

I remember somebody telling me he couldn't understand why grown men put themselves through that kind of pressure. And I wasn't sure I understood it, either.

Bump

4

"COACH," A REPORTER innocently asked me early in 1974, "do you know what people are saying?"

"No. What?"

"They're saying this is really going to be your first team at Arizona State. That those great records the last two years were accomplished with Winkles players."

"Boy," I thought, "there it is again. Bobby gets all the credit for the sixty-four and fifty-nine wins, but I get all the blame for the six and eight losses."

Then the reporter asked, "How do you feel about what people are saying?"

Actually, in a way, I felt pretty good. I was anxious to show people what I could do. There wasn't a single player on the 1974 team that had ever played an inning for Bobby Winkles, and I was glad to get to the point where it was finally going to be my team—although it was a shame to get there with a club so young and inexperienced. I would be starting as many as four freshmen, and this was obviously going to be one of the youngest clubs ASU had ever had. The lack of acceptance by the fans still stung. So did the criticism over the Bane decision. I had always reacted very badly to any kind of criticism. I just couldn't handle it and either got violently angry or depressed or both.

Don't get me wrong. Many of the players on those first two ASU teams had been very good to me. Bane, for instance, was great from the very first day, when he gave my wife his seat at the press conference. But my feeling was always that I would never really be their coach. No matter how much they accepted me, their guru had left. I would never be as funny as Winkles; they would never like me as much as Winkles. I pictured the players as well as the fans sitting around telling old Winkles stories. I remember one incident the first season when a player came in after misplaying a ball in the outfield. I was standing in front of the dugout talking quietly with him, and I heard some fans saying Bobby never would have done it that way. He would have waited until the player got down into the dugout. In fact, Ed Wiggins of the *Mesa Tribune*, a good friend of mine from way back, warned me that things like that were going to be misinterpreted.

Nevertheless, in spite of The Giant Shadow, the bitter taste of the Bane incident, and the recent unpleasantness at Omaha, 1974 started on an upbeat note.

We were young, but we'd had a super recruiting year. There seemed to be no end to the stream of talent coming in—players like Floyd Bannister and Kenny Landreaux. Fall is a strange time in college baseball. You play mostly intrasquad games, and it's not always easy to tell how much you're accomplishing. Still, we obviously had some exciting young players, and they seemed to be improving.

But there is no getting around inexperience. In college baseball, the flowers that bloom in the fall sometimes wilt a little in the spring. The Devils got away from the gate at 7-5, and the papers gloomily took note of the fact it was the worst Arizona State start in a decade. What made it worse was that all five losses were at home. As I look back, the team was as shaky as I was. It was a young team that needed patience, needed to be brought along slowly, needed minimizing of losses, needed encouragement. Instead, I did just the opposite.

Tightening the screws was what had always worked for me in the past when things started to slip. So I tightened the screws again. The pressure on me was great, and I took it right out on the field and put it on the kids.

"My God, you lost again!" I would scream. "You guys are absolutely the worst I've ever been around." We went to long practices, accompanied by a great deal of running, and my sarcasm went from cutesy to biting.

It didn't seem to do much good at first, but then we went over to Riverside, California, where we'd lost

43

with two great clubs before, and this time we played pretty well. We ended up winning the tournament. Of course, Southern Cal wasn't in it that year, but still I felt pretty good. Intimidation had worked again, the kids had been tempered by the fire and were ready. The only thing that worried me a little bit was that the University of Arizona was also off to a good start.

The Devils opened WAC play in El Paso and then came home to play three games against New Mexico. Since we never lost to the University of Texas at El Paso anywhere and hardly ever lost to the Lobos in Tempe, prospects for a 6-0 conference start seemed very bright. The timing of the schedule couldn't have been better, I thought. We had come into our own, and we were ready.

Arizona State lost the opener at El Paso. It was like Russia losing to Poland in chess. We took a lead into the eighth inning and blew it.

We bounced back to sweep a doubleheader the next day, but that didn't really undo the damage, since a loss to the Miners was considered grounds for losing not only the championship but Arizona residency as well. However, bad as things were, the UTEP series very shortly seemed like good times.

We came back home to play three nonconference games against La Verne College. It has a fine small college program, but they didn't really figure to give us much of a problem. In fact, it looked like a pretty good chance to get our momentum going again. We had recently moved from Sun Devil Field to Packard

Stadium, and the field was not yet in good shape. Neither was the weather. Playing conditions were terrible, and so were we. We lost all three games—badly.

It was the most miserable three games I can remember. We had now lost four games out of six, three straight at home, and were behind by a very big game in the WAC standings.

Somebody once said that in sports everything is always magnified—the good times are not as good as they seem, and the bad times are not as bad. Maybe! But I felt I had reached a career low. With things this bad, I didn't get along with the players, the coaches, or my wife. I had only one answer—yell louder, cuss louder, intimidate more.

The last La Verne game ended at about six o'clock. I called the players together, told them they were a gutless bunch of dogs, that they weren't going to play that way for me, and that they were going to run until my arm got too tired to wave them around. I said I hoped a lot of them would quit, and that when it was over, maybe we'd have nine people left who wanted to play college baseball. Then I ran them. Every mile or two, I'd stop them and remind them how miserable they were, and I kept it up until after dark. Players threw up, and some got cramps, but nobody quit. Finally, after two hours, I called a halt.

Feeling that they still needed a little more fear to take home with them, I made them a promise: "If you think what happened tonight was bad, wait until you see what's going to happen tomorrow night."

I had no idea what it was going to be, of course, but it was going to be rough.

That night at home I probably didn't say five words all night, and my wife didn't try to get any more out of me. She knew if I wanted to talk, I'd say something. I didn't. I didn't sleep well, either, and didn't actually decide on what particular drill I was going to run until I got to the park that night.

Packard Stadium had been irrigated, so we had to practice at Rendezvous Park in Mesa, where we were going to open the New Mexico series the next night. The field was hard. I knew that better than anybody, but I decided on a hit-and-run drill, with me hitting the ball into right field and the players taking off from first, sprinting around second, and sliding into third.

In my mind I thought I'd run everybody through it three or four times, but as things went along, the players really seemed to be doing well. They were running scared and sliding hard. They had started to respond; they had finally gotten the word, so I was fairly happy. I had done it again—the old Brock magic had worked.

As they were completing the third round, I thought maybe it was time for me to get out of the way, to loosen the yoke a bit. The punishment was over. The atrocities had ended. By this time, I was standing over by third watching the sliding. As I looked up, Bump Wills, the last player in the group, was rounding second. Bump was a 100-percent ballplayer, the one bright spot in the whole mess, and I never had blamed any of our shortcomings on him. I put up my hands and yelled, "Okay, that's enough. Let's go to the hitting drill," and turned away.

But at that moment, Bump was already starting his slide. He spike caught, his ankle went under, and there was an unbelievable scream. It was all so ironic, because Bump was a superb slider. He must have inherited it from his father, Maury Wills, who stole so many bases for the Los Angeles Dodgers. But there he was, screaming and rolling over. And you could sense the immediate reaction from the other players: "Look what that —— coach has done to Bump."

After he was carried off on a stretcher, we went on with practice for probably a half hour, and I remember that Garrett Strong, a guy Bump helped recruit, was so mad he hit five out of the park in batting practice. Actually, Bump was popular with all the players. There was a mystique about him that made him a little bit different from everybody else. Part of it was his father. But most of it was Bump himself.

Troy Young, our trainer, said he thought Bump's ankle was broken. After practice, I called the team together for a little talk. I don't think I took the blame completely at the time, but I alluded to it. The talk was half "these things happen" and half "I went a little too far." I left it at that and headed for home. I didn't ride on the bus, so the players had some time together.

Bump Wills had been something of a disappointment his second season as a Sun Devil, but he did start in left field. By 1974, he had blossomed into a brilliant second baseman with a great big-league career stretching ahead of him.

Young's assessment of the injury proved correct— it was an ugly break, and Bump was to play no baseball for many months. However, there were no permanent ill effects (except a little pain when it rains). In fact, when Bump returned to baseball, he was clocked faster going to first base than before the injury, and he went on to win a starting job with the Texas Rangers.

But I had no way of knowing that as I drove home that night. All I could see was that my policy of intimidation and my desire to win at all costs had ruined a young man's career, and that everybody in the world would stomp on me tomorrow. I would almost certainly be fired, if not executed. Actually, while my concern for Bump was genuine, I was also working on what had all the makings of a terminal case of self-pity.

I decided to stop by Fred's house before I went home. I figured he was the guy who was going to fire me, and I didn't want him to do it at least until I had a chance to talk to him. Fred doesn't usually over-react. In fact, he generally underreacts, and that's what he did this time, although not quite as much as I'd hoped. He did say the thought of firing his base-ball coach had never crossed his mind. I hung some hope on that. The main advice he gave me was not to blame myself and certainly not to tell anybody I thought it was my fault.

Dr. Fred's advice was, of course, very sound, but the fear and guilt I felt that night were overpowering. Before long, those feelings were joined by two more: despair and anger. I was down, as far down as I could ever remember being. The longest, darkest night of my life was underway.

The Long Night

5

As I DROVE HOME from Fred's house, my mood vacillated between anger and self-pity. Sure it was a terrible misfortune, I told myself, but it wasn't really my fault. Those donkeys couldn't do anything right.

I also convinced myself that it didn't make any difference. My job had been to serve as a buffer so the coach who followed me at ASU would have some kind of a chance. He wouldn't have to live under the Winkles shadow. Now my job was about over ... and on I went.

I'm a classic worrier and pessimist, and Pat and I had a standard joke about it. If we had a sixty-five-game schedule and we had won the opener, I'd say, "Well, the worst we can be for the season is one and sixty-four." While we laughed about it, there was some truth to it, and it revealed my deeper feelings. I always saw the dark side of everything—we won today, but we might never win again. That's how I felt as I pulled into the driveway.

Pat had seen me down before. After all, I'd handled coming in second at Omaha very poorly. But she'd never seen me anywhere near as down as I was that night.

I had talked off and on for years about getting out of coaching, but, although Pat was my partner in every sense of the word, she had never been a party to that plan. She always argued that I had to keep coaching, that it was the only thing that would ever make me happy. She thought I could really contribute to the guys, that they would be better off down the road for having played for me, etc., etc. I never bought that, and besides, even if it were true, that wasn't what was important to me.

She was always my faithful supporter. In my first six years as head coach, Arizona State played more than 400 baseball games. And though she had a full-time job of her own, she missed no more than five or six of those games—home or away. In fact, if you count the times I was thrown out, she'd probably seen more ASU baseball than I had. And, in addition to her job teaching in college, she'd been practically a full-time unpaid member of the university staff, serving as an academic advisor, personal appointments secretary, assistant on recruiting trips, and operator of what amounted to a year-round, we-never-close open house and smorgasbord for the players.

When I was recruiting at Mesa College one year, I spent a little more money than the school budget allowed. Instead of providing dorm space for a couple of the players, I had them move in with us. I don't think there's been a time since then when we haven't had a player or two or half a dozen around the house. Pat has looked on my coaching as sort of a family business. Brock & Brock, Inc., Baseball and Education. The funny thing is, I don't think she'd ever seen a baseball game until she came to one when I was coaching my second Legion team.

Now, as I told Pat in very sharp terms what had happened at practice, she tried desperately to find the right thing to say. She had a knack for it, even though I didn't always recognize the truth of what she said at the time. I remember when Jerry Kindall and I were running for the University of Arizona job and he got it. I was really down on the way home from Tucson, and Pat said, "Cheer up. Things always work out for the best, and there's some reason why you didn't get the job."

"Sure," I said, "they gave it to a guy who's never coached a victory in his life, just because he was a big league ball player. They're going to be sorry."

But Pat wouldn't let go. "How do you know what's going to happen tomorrow? Maybe Bobby Winkles will resign at Arizona State, and you'll have a shot at that job."

I turned and ended all conversation for the rest of that trip by telling her that was the stupidest thing I'd ever heard anybody say. If she couldn't think of anything smarter to say, she should keep quiet.

The next morning Bobby Winkles told me privately that he was talking to the California Angels and would probably take a job with them. Three days later, he resigned at Arizona State. So Pat was right in more ways than one. (I was wrong in more ways than one, too. Four years after he took the Arizona job, Jerry Kindall led the Wildcats to their first NCAA baseball championship.)

That night, however, nothing that Pat said helped. I had tried a beer at Fred's house, and it hadn't done anything for me, so I tried another beer at home. That didn't help either. It made me mad that I couldn't even drink, and I crushed the can and threw it across the kitchen.

Pat responded the way she always did, telling me that things couldn't really be that bad. When I exploded, she knew enough to stay away from me, leaving me to sink deeper and deeper into self-pity and guilt at having ruined the career of Bump Wills.

I really liked Bump. He was not only a key man on the team, but he was the only player I felt close to. I was concerned about what he'd think, and I didn't want him to hate me.

Bump had a stuttering problem, and when I was younger, I'd had one, too. Each time I answered the phone, met a new person, or spoke in front of a group, it had been an ordeal. I still cringe when I think about those painful, humiliating moments. I suppose that was one reason I took a special interest in Bump. I knew from my own experience what he was going through.

I had also disciplined Bump in his junior year. He

had had a bad year both in school and on the field. I overheard his girl friend talk about an all-night drinking party the night before a game, so I made him run miles. I found out later that Bump hadn't been involved, but had gotten out of bed to quiet things down when some of the guys at the fraternity house got a little rowdy.

At that time, he told me he was going to quit school and try to make a fresh start by signing with a pro ball club. I tried to change his mind, but nothing I said could persuade him.

Finally he said to me, "Why should I stay in school? Give me one reason."

I had said everything at that point, so I asked him to stay as a favor to me. To my surprise, he said he would.

A year later, with his ankle broken, I knew I had to see him. Pat and I drove over to the university infirmary that evening and I choked up when I saw him lying there.

"I'm sorry," I began. "It's my fault. I'll always know it's my fault."

"Do me a favor," Bump asked. "Don't *ever* think it was your fault. As long as you live, don't consider it your fault. I could have broken it going down stairs."

I wasn't sure I could do that favor, but I felt my visit was at least a slight encouragement to Bump, and it lifted my spirits ever so slightly. But Pat and I were both subdued when we got back home.

Neither of us got much sleep that night. I tossed and turned, but finally got up around 5:30 A.M., at which point a thoroughly worried Pat could think of only one thing to say:

"Why don't you stop and see Pastor Davidson?"

"If he doesn't fix broken ankles, what possible good is he to me?" I shot back.

Pat answered weakly, "Well ... stop by anyway."

That was too much for me. I stormed out the front door and headed for my car.

As ridiculous as the statement sounded to me at the time, I accepted it as the natural thing for her to say. The daughter of a carpenter and part-time Church of Christ minister from Mayfield, Kentucky, Pat had always been, I assumed, a Christian. She believed in it, and she really wanted a church relationship. I never really bought the whole church scene, and it had been something of a bone of contention between us. I just didn't think it was important. It was as though I had a list of twenty priorities, and religion was number twenty-one.

A few minutes after I stormed out, I came back to pick up something I'd forgotten. Our marriage, like most successful partnerships, had seen good times and not-so-good times. But never, not even in the worst of times, had I ever parted from Pat on a to-heck-with-everything note. But I came very, very close to it this time.

"When will I see you?" she called as I headed back out the door.

"If I'm still around," I snapped back, "I'll see you at noon." And I drove off into the dawn.

It was 5:47 A.M. on Good Friday.

58

This Was My Life

6

OFTEN IN THE PAST when the pressure got too great, I would just climb in my car and drive . . . nowhere in particular, just drive. This time, however, I found myself following a route I knew all too well—the route my life had taken for thirty-seven years.

The first nineteen years I'd spent at 4016 North 4th Street in Phoenix. I parked the car not too far from the old house and sat.

It was a place with many happy memories for me, mostly because of the very unusual relationship I'd had with my dad. I loved him much more than the average son loves the average father; we were about as tight-knit as could be. But we argued about everything. I would scream at him, and he would scream at me, and we'd shock people. They didn't realize that we both enjoyed it very much. Even when I was furious with him, I was aware of how much he loved me. Every action he took, everything he did, was for

61

me. I was his whole life. When he finally died, I was crushed, and it took me a long time to recover.

As far as I'm concerned, William Davis Brock, Sr., deserves a book of his own. His discharge from the service in 1926 listed his health as "very poor," and his respiratory problems (which included the loss of a lung) never got any better. With the exception of a brief period after World War II, he had no job. He supported the family with a small government pension and the rent from three apartments behind our home.

He went on spitting and snarling at the world for forty more years before finally giving in. He dedicated those years almost exclusively to helping me and, in the process, thousands of other Valley youngsters. Poor health and all, my dad almost single-handedly financed, supervised, badgered, bullied, cussed, and sometimes even folded, spindled, and mutilated one of the most successful American Legion baseball programs in the United States. And he didn't spill a single drop of sweetness along the way.

Dad didn't yell just at relatives. He yelled at friends, enemies, strangers, everybody. He was the wrath that turned away soft answers.

He was always battling somebody about something. A lot of the time he was wrong, but a lot of the time he was right, too. He was fiery, hostile, and antireligious; he loved any kind of a fight. I remember when people used to call the house for rulings on Legion controversies. He never tried to smooth things over. He raised a lot of money for Legion ball after the slot machines that had been financing the program were declared illegal. He came up with a Keep Good Boys Good Club and sold memberships for something like $19.88, which is what he figured it cost to keep one boy playing one year. He was one of those guys who really fought people and was mean. But, strangely, when you came right down to it, almost everybody loved him.

I thought of my mother, too, Elsie, a gentle, loving, quiet woman, the nicest in the whole world. Whenever dad and I would have one of our terrible fights, she was always around to pick up the pieces. She had been a nurse until a severe arthritic condition made it difficult for her to get around.

Mom used to make my sister, Tommy Lou, and me go to Sunday school at Bethel Methodist Church. She's seven years older than I am, and she didn't want to be there, either. Later, when she was about nineteen or twenty, she became a Christian, and it turned her life around completely. Then she was always scheming and praying to get me anyplace where I might be exposed to the gospel. She's handled her share of life's problems with tremendous love and patience, and if there are any saints walking the earth, she's among them.

The Sunday school teacher was a man named Lance Durhamm, who also happened to be my elementary school principal. He was nice enough, but he was still my principal, and the whole experience didn't exactly thrill me.

After I turned sixteen, one of my jobs was to take

mother to the old First Baptist Church in Phoenix when she felt well enough to go. Most of the time, however, I spent my growing-up years playing whatever sport happened to be in season. School, in the beginning, was no big deal. As long as I passed, that was good enough for dad. In fact, I can remember him actually making fun of kids who got good grades. But I can also remember that when they were going to hold me back in the second grade, he went down to the school and hollered and screamed and carried on until they finally promoted me. Dad used to sort of imply he'd gotten through high school, but I later learned he actually didn't make it past the sixth grade. But I have seldom known a brighter or more knowledgeable man. He eventually became very obsessed with me completing college.

My early academic problems were more emotional than intellectual. My stuttering was severe. I had a hard time saying my own name, which always made the opening of class something of a trauma.

In a way, the problem helped steer me into an athletic career. Even at a very early age, I was extremely competitive. I seemed driven. I *had* to excel at something. And, as it happens, the one thing I did better than most of my schoolmates was play ball.

It was hard for me in those days to be much more than an average student, because my stutter kept me from doing so many things. But on the ball field, I not only could excel, but I didn't stutter. When I got into athletics, it really turned my dad on.

The first experience I can remember came when I was twelve and went out for a Class C team. I made it and probably would have been one of the top three pitchers. But dad was afraid maybe I wouldn't get to pitch enough, and, besides, some of my friends hadn't made the team. So he hunted around and dug up a sponsor, fielded a team of his own, and we won quite a few games.

This forged the father-son link that was to span four decades and influence not only my future but that of baseball in Arizona. Having conquered Class C, we moved on to Legion baseball.

Over long stretches, my dad had to spend quite a bit of time in bed, and one of my classic memories is of the summer he had a friend build a framed canvas with a strike zone painted on it outside his window. He also had a mound built, and bought about five dozen baseballs. I would try to throw strikes at the canvas, and he would lie by the window offering encouragement. I was small and on the frail side and didn't throw hard at all. But I could hit that strike zone pretty regularly and had a decent curve.

Dad was absolutely convinced that anybody who could throw strikes like I could would make it to the big leagues, but he really didn't have much of a baseball background. In fact, he didn't really do the coaching on his teams. He would make the moves, all right, but usually he would ask me first. So at thirteen I was already "coaching."

Dad's absolute certainty of my Hall of Fame future triggered at least a thousand of the one million arguments (those are single-season, not career to-tals) we had. He wouldn't let me go out for football because he was afraid I'd be permanently injured and ruin my baseball career. He started telling me that in the fifth grade. He said basketball was okay, but my coaches cut me because I was too short. I had pretty good insight for a youngster, and, although I was winning a lot of games and making a lot of all-star teams, by fifteen I was acutely aware of my missing fast ball. I think I would have been better off if I hadn't known. Sometimes it's easier to exceed your limitations if you don't know what they are, and I probably could have played a little pro ball. I had one chance to sign with the Red Sox organization, but it didn't work out.

I lived for the summers in Arizona, but because of coaching, not playing. I remember the night it really came down to a choice between the two. The Legion B team I was coaching and the semi-pro team I was playing for had games at the same time, and I didn't hesitate a minute to choose coaching over playing. Dad didn't give up his dream right away, but later, when he finally saw what I wanted, he got off the playing bandwagon and on the coaching bandwagon.

He was always changing to keep up with my plans. When I got out of high school, I wanted to go to the University of Arizona. Coach Frank Sancet wanted me but didn't offer any aid, and I definitely couldn't go down there without any help. So dad worked all summer trying to get me a scholarship at Arizona State. Baseball wasn't a very big deal there then. In fact, one of the football assistants was the head baseball coach. Anyway, dad, with help from Ben Foote of the *Phoenix Gazette,* finally got me the scholarship.

I went over to Tempe for Frosh Week, but I hated it and called dad and told him I wasn't going to be happy there at all. So he got on the phone to Johnny Riggs, then the baseball coach at Phoenix College, and I played there for two years.

Riggs was a tremendous man who was really concerned about what happened to his players, and he liked me a lot. He went into administration after my first year, and the basketball coach, Runt Goddard, handled baseball the second year. Then I got another scholarship to ASU but never played much there. By this time I was married and we had a baby, and I needed to go to work, so I started umpiring high-school ball every night.

... And now another ballplayer about the same age as I had been—but with infinitely more talent—lay in a hospital bed grimacing with pain and wondering if his career were finished.

A Friday Morning Miracle

7

IT WAS NEARLY DAYLIGHT by the time I drove past the old Osborn Elementary School—or, at least, what had been the old school. It was a financial center now. At Osborn I had met Joe DeWitt, who had a tremendous influence on my career.

Joe was my seventh-grade teacher and my coach. He was good-looking, and I thought he was very cool. I really looked up to Joe. As a result I started thinking I might like to be a physical education teacher and coach. . . .

The morning rush hour was well on when I nosed my Monte Carlo past North High School. North was always a very special place to me. I started my public-school coaching career there as a jayvee coach and ended up 16-2. I loved every minute of that. And, of course, I played at North. Shanty Hogan was the coach, and I think I learned more baseball from him in my junior year than in any other year of my career. I didn't try any volunteer coaching that year. Shanty handled it all.

71

But my senior year he left to become head football coach at the new South High School, and Paul McCloy succeeded him. Paul was very nice, but, well, it was back to "coaching." I used to think the top of my career would be to become the head baseball coach at North High School, and one of my biggest thrills to this day was being named student of the week there.

It was at North High School that I began dating the captain of the cheerleaders, an exceptionally friendly and bright girl named Pat Futrell. Pat was good for me from the beginning. When I came to her house, she'd ask, "Where are your books?"

"Books?"

My study habits improved perceptibly, and we became inseparable. I was a freshman at Phoenix College by then and she was a junior at North. She didn't plan to go to college, so we figured that if she went to work, and I held enough part-time jobs, we could get married right after her graduation. Then we figured we could get married before graduation if we saved enough to live on until then.

My dad, however, would have no part of that. He believed no one should get married until they'd saved enough to pay cash for their house, furniture, and car. Since I was a few dollars short, he screamed a lot. He was also afraid I wouldn't finish college. No Brock, to our knowledge, had ever gone that far, and he wanted me to break that streak.

A year earlier, when I told him I wanted to give Pat a ring, he'd growled, "Okay, if you can pay cash for it." I did, but when I told him about it, he acted as though we had played a dirty trick on him.

At first Dad had threatened that he wouldn't go to the wedding, but he did. Then he said that was it. Don't come to him for another thing. Not one penny, even if we were starving. As a matter of fact, it was nearly twenty-four hours after the wedding before he lifted a finger to help us.

We were married on May 10, 1956, at the Mountain View Church of Christ in North Phoenix. We honeymooned at romantic Hi Corbett Field in Tucson, where the state high school tournament was being held. Some of the players on my Legion team were there, and baseball became part of our marriage from day one.

Dad, for all his bark, liked Pat, and they became very close. I don't think he ever yelled at her. The two of them worked together to help me get whatever I wanted, but there was never any jealousy. . . .

The sun and the thermometer had started to climb by the time I reached West High that morning. That was where I had gotten my first teaching position. I taught driver education and coached freshman baseball.

By now, I had made it clear across the Valley and found myself driving past the first house Pat and I had together. We had lived briefly with dad, but true to form, I'd had a big argument with him, and we'd decided on a place of our own.

Driving past the scenes of my life wasn't helping my depression, however. Even revisiting the happy times of my youth didn't seem to help much, but I drove on, this time back on the other side of the Valley to Mesa.

Mesa High School was where I reached the first goal I had thought would make me happy—head baseball coach. On the way into Mesa, I drove past old Scottsdale Field, where I coached my first game, the one in which Jim Palmer hit the towering home run to beat us 1-0. I spent two years at Mesa, had a 12-6 record the first year, won the conference the second, and lost 1-0 in the state tournament. That was a happy time.

It was nearing mid-morning as I drove past the original site of Mesa Community College, or, as it was called then, Mesa Extension of Phoenix College. That was my first rung on the college coaching ladder. We called it Someday Junior College . . . someday, it would amount to something. Baseball there was really a glorified jayvee program at first, but it was college. I'd spent seven years at Mesa College and worked very hard. It was a happy time, too, especially the first three years.

By the time I left Mesa College, the HoKams were a national power not only in baseball but football and track as well. The school had moved to a spacious new campus. John Riggs, who had helped me earlier, was the first executive dean at MCC. In his fourth year there, I was named chairman of the physical-education department, which, I thought, was the beginning of some kind of administrative career.

If MCC gave me my first real taste of glory, it also gave me the first glimpse of the grief that had reduced me to driving the streets of the Valley that Good Friday morning in search of who-knew-what. We won back-to-back national titles at MCC, but I also made the very unfortunate discovery that the worse I treated the players, the better the results—at least on the scoreboard.

Much of my anger was gone by this time, but I was still feeling sorry for myself. I was also a little tired of driving and had no idea where to go next. Should I go to the hospital and see Bump? Should I stop and see that pastor Pat had mentioned? Instead, I pulled off the road and went nowhere. For a long time I just sat.

I had three basic feelings. Fear was very strong, the terrible fear of what was going to happen to me . . . being called into Dr. Miller's office and being fired . . . visions of bad press. I was afraid I was going to lose my integrity, my reputation, and my job. There wasn't going to be anything left at all.

The second feeling was shame. I had always felt time was the great healer, but how could I ever face Bump again? What if he couldn't play? And even if he could, there was no way I'd ever be able to completely erase the shame of what I'd done to him.

Finally, there was hopelessness . . . a strong sense of hopelessness. There was no hope for Bump, no hope for forgiveness for what I'd done because of my desire to get the team ready for the New Mexico series at any cost. No hope of forestalling the disastrous chain of events that was about to occur because of that stupid sliding drill. It all added up to total despair.

By this time, I was back on the road again, and suddenly I noticed I was near the church of the pastor Pat had mentioned.

Actually, Guy Davidson's name wasn't really that much of a red flag to me. He was the pastor of Tempe's Grace Community Church, but I knew him through a small Optimist Club in which we both were charter members. He didn't seem like a minister to me. He wasn't preachy or stuffy, as I thought most were. He was just someone you could talk to. I also liked the way he had handled himself when he'd visited our house. When we'd told him to buzz off because we liked to sleep late on Sunday mornings, he buzzed off. He didn't tell us we were going to perish in the flames of hell or anything like that.

Strangely enough, I learned later that Pat had lived next door to him as a child. His parents and hers had been very close friends, and her initials were carved in the back porch of his house.

I didn't think Guy Davidson could do much to help me, however. No one had died. I wasn't facing divorce. I had none of the problems you usually take to a minister. I doubted he could understand. Someone had broken an ankle. So what? Write that down on paper, and it doesn't sound so bad. Davidson wasn't a baseball man. Could he ever grasp the seriousness of the situation, the fact that perhaps my job, my career, all I'd worked for all my life was in jeopardy?

I think what prompted me to stop the car there was

my concern for my relationship with Pat. Things hadn't been going too well. Probably I'd been rough on her and I thought that talking to this pastor would make her think I was trying. She felt so strongly that I should talk to someone, and Davidson was her only suggestion.

It was early, and I thought, "He's probably not there yet anyhow. I'll just go up and knock and come right back. Then I can tell Pat I tried." When I realized how silly that was, I started the car again to drive off, but the fact was I didn't have any place to go. I certainly didn't want to go to the office where everyone would ask about Bump. I had talked to Fred, and he couldn't help me. I had tried drinking, and that did nothing. So I switched off the motor, walked the few steps to the church and knocked on the door that read, "Pastor's Office."

He was in, and in a few minutes I found myself sitting opposite him, wondering what in the world I'd say. Finally I blurted out the whole story.

Guy Davidson hadn't heard about the accident, and he was interested. He listened while I tried to paint the seriousness of the picture, and I felt, surprisingly, that he understood. When he began to talk, he said nothing about coming to church or any of the things I had feared he might.

Instead, he asked me if I knew Jesus Christ as my Lord and Savior. He talked about a relationship with a person . . . about Jesus Christ as someone I could know, could talk to . . . a friend . . . someone who could take care of the problems I couldn't handle.

77

Frankly, I had never heard it that way. I believed Jesus Christ was God. I believed the Bible was true—except for a few places, perhaps, where it seemed a little strict according to my standards, and I assumed that something had been lost in the translation there.

We had joined a church in Mesa years ago, and on the first Sunday when I opened the hymnal, there inside the back cover were the rules. You can't do this; you can't do that. It was what I expected, and my resolution to follow them lasted about two weeks.

Now, the thought of someone who could take this enormous weight off my back was startlingly new. The person of Jesus Christ appeared to be on my side. He wasn't the great enforcer of rules, however. He was a super-powerful, totally faithful Friend who I knew would be there no matter how badly I messed up.

When Guy Davidson said, "Jim, you've tried everything else. Isn't it time you gave Jesus Christ a chance?" I was ready. I knew he was right.

Then Davidson read a verse from the Bible: "Look, I have been standing at the door and constantly knocking. If anyone hears me calling him and opens the door, I will come in and fellowship with him and he with me."

That meant, he explained, that if I would simply yield my life to Jesus Christ, let him take over and be the Lord, he would care for any problems I ever had.

Jesus Christ was there in that office on the morning of Good Friday. He put his arms around me saying, "Hey, I know you've got problems. Don't worry! I can help. Tell me about them. I'm waiting. I care."

In that instant my fear, my guilt, and my hopelessness were gone.

Just like that? Could a thirty-minute chat with a minister completely change a man's life? Could a new perspective on the image of God instantly wipe out the deadly depression and self-imposed guilt that had driven me all over the Valley and back over my entire life that long morning? Could it suddenly relieve the pressures that had nearly driven me out of coaching time and time again for years?

I have to answer, yes. I had walked into Pastor Guy Davidson's office that Good Friday morning in 1974 as a basket case. I walked out as a serene and confident man. In my mind it's easy to explain. What happened was a miracle.

A Rookie Coach

8

WHEN I LEFT THE PASTOR'S OFFICE, I was a little unsure of my next move. Somehow I knew things were going to be different, but I wasn't quite clear on exactly how, or what I was supposed to do. Although I was a veteran baseball coach, I was pretty much of a rookie in the Christian league.

I still had almost two hours before I was supposed to meet Pat for lunch, and for some reason I got to thinking about the financial problem I'd been having with the Maricopa County Junior College District. While at Mesa, I had taken a paid leave to work on that doctorate. Their rule was that if you came back to work for at least two semesters, you didn't owe the district anything. But, of course, the ASU baseball job came up, and I never went back to Mesa even for a day. So they wanted me to return the $7,800 they had paid me while I wasn't working. I'd been fighting them, and my lawyer and I had reason to believe I

83

could get out of it partly because of work I had done for Mesa while on leave.

Suddenly I realized I was now governed by a different set of rules. It was no longer a matter of what my lawyer could get me out of, but what was right and wrong.

I drove to the district office in downtown Phoenix, walked in, and told a very surprised assistant to the president that I wanted to acknowledge my debt and work out some kind of payment plan. The school people were relieved, because the issue was becoming very sticky. My lawyer wasn't relieved, though. "You dumb so-and-so," he said later. "How could you do such a thing? We had them." But I knew I had done the right thing and I was glad.

Pat was waiting for me at noon when I pulled up in front of the Bull and Barrel Restaurant in Scottsdale. I'm sure I surprised her with the way I bounced out of the car and hurried toward her.

"Hey, don't worry. Everything is going to be fine."

I fed back to her almost the same lines she had left me with eight hours before, and it startled her. That was the last thing she expected. I could see she was relieved, and she wanted to know what had happened, but all I could tell her at the moment was that I had met with Pastor Davidson and it had gone well. It just didn't seem like the time and the place to tell the whole story.

I didn't understand all that was happening myself, and I wasn't sure that she would. Certain standards, certain values and ideas stood out clearly now. I knew something had changed in my life, that I would never be the old Jim Brock again, but I couldn't explain it all. Pat was happy enough that the man who had slammed the door in despair early that morning now appeared to be on top of the world. She didn't probe.

After lunch I stopped by the old Sun Devil Field to watch a few innings of a jayvee game and bumped into Doug Slocum, a sliderballing righthander who had earned junior college All-American honors while leading my last Mesa team to a national title. Everyone had expected Slocum to be the ace of the ASU staff his senior year, but his elbow had locked in his first game. Surgery had been necessary to correct the problem, and he never was able to pitch much, but he was now the Sun Devil captain.

Doug had always been very protective of me and would minimize or try to cover up any dissension or criticism of me on the team. Like Pat, he was always assuring me everything was just fine. So I asked him what was the squad reaction to Bump's injury.

"Coach," he said, "we're in big trouble. Most of the players blame you for what happened, and there's talk of getting up a petition to get you fired. There's just tremendous resentment."

It didn't really surprise me. I'd been kicking the players around, and this was their chance to kick back. It didn't bother me, either. For some reason, I had every confidence things were going to work out and told Doug as much, which was certainly a reversal of our usual roles.

About the time Doug and I were talking, a group of the players went to visit Bump. His attitude was critical to the future of my life. If he'd been lying there grumbling about what that so-and-so had done to him, I would have been in deep trouble. But Bump told them what he had said to me the night before. It was just one of those things; he didn't blame me a bit. His attitude toward me hadn't faltered, and never has. He has always been tremendously friendly and supportive. Here was a guy in his senior year and on the verge of being drafted very high who was suddenly flat on his back, but there was never a trace of bitterness.

I'd been worried about what his dad would say, too. But Maury's only comment was he'd been around baseball a hundred years and things like this were part of the game.

By the time I got on the team bus that night to go to the Lobo opener, I sensed a change in attitude. The long faces and bitter looks I might have expected weren't there. The players who'd visited the hospital had obviously spread the word, "Hey, Bump says it wasn't coach's fault." Everybody seemed to have accepted what happened. I was very much under control and simply said, "Let's go beat the Lobos."

We did, too. We beat them about as badly as La-Verne had beaten us the first part of the week: 10-0.

Late that evening, I was sitting and just thinking about the tremendous events of that day when I remembered I'd been invited to a breakfast the next morning. A Christian organization called Campus

Crusade is very active on the State campus, and a young man named Roger Gehring worked with them. He had been given the simple assignment of converting all of the Arizona State athletes to Christianity. As soon as he got that done, I'm sure they had something else in mind for him. Roger had a certain boldness, which I later learned was something that only the Holy Spirit can give you. At the time, I thoughtt Roger was totally obnoxious. He was there all the time, asking me survey questions on my God-image. I though he was a bore, and I tried to avoid him.

About a month before, I had walked into my office one morning, and Roger, who had been hiding behind the file cabinet, leaped out.

"Who let you in here, Roger?" I snarled.

He said, "Coach, I'm so excited, I know you will be too when I tell you. It's really exciting news."

I said, "What, you're leaving town?"

"No, no, coach," he said. "On the Saturday morning before Easter, we're going to get sixty athletes together for a big breakfast to meet Jim King. Wouldn't you just want to be there and hear that?"

"Yea, Rog, that would really be super. However, I am tied up that Saturday."

"No," he said. "I looked at your calendar as I was waiting for you. That date's empty."

The easiest thing to do at that point was to lie to Roger and tell him I'd be there. That's what I did. I didn't know where I'd be on that Saturday, but I had no intention of ever going to that silly breakfast.

After he left, I called my secretary and said, "Lucille, you see the Bible-thumping Jesus freak walking out that door?"

"Yes, coach."

I said, "The next time he catches me in my office, you're fired."

I found out later that Lucille was a Christian and had been working with Roger all along.

I had put the incident completely out of my mind until that Friday night. Now I wanted to attend the breakfast with the same intensity that I had wanted to avoid it before.

"Jim King is a Christian coach," I thought. "Now I'm one of those. I've been one for about twelve hours. That would be exciting to hear him."

I got up early the next morning and drove to the Student Union. Roger was taking tickets as I walked in, and I could see he was surprised.

"Oh, coach, you made it," he mumbled.

I said, "Roger, can I talk to you for a minute?" I'm sure he thought I was going to tell him I could stay only five minutes or something.

"You know, Roger," I began, "I don't know just how tightly this is planned today, but would there be a chance for me to address the group?"

Roger, I learned later, has a lot of faith, but he turned white as a sheet and said, "You want to do what?"

"I'd like to talk to the group."

He hesitated. "Our time schedule is tight."

I said, "Roger, I put you off for a long time. I don't

The 1949 baseball season was the first ever for 12-year-old Jimmy Brock. He's standing second from the left in the back row.

Young Jim Brock accepts the plaque for his 1957 American Legion state championship team, while his proud father looks over his shoulder.

In his first game as a college coach, Jim Brock lasted only three innings before being ejected by major league umpire Stan Landis.

In the years preceding 1974, conversations such as these were a trademark of Coach Brock's style.

Prior to a 1973 exhibition game between Arizona State and the California Angels, Jim Brock and Bobby Winkles go over ground rules with the umpires. Brock had discovered that Winkles, his predecessor at ASU, was a tough act to follow.

Bump Wills (below) takes a pitch during a 1973 ball game. The next year, an accident during a sliding drill would finish his college baseball career and nearly wreck Jim Brock's. Wills recovered and went on to play second base for the American League Texas Rangers. He sent his college coach this picture (right) of himself and his famous base-stealing father, Maury Wills.

To Jim and Pat: with affection and gratitude

During the predawn hours of the day following the Bump Wills accident, Coach Brock wandered off, alone with his depression. This photo, taken from the movie The Devils' Coach *(Outreach Films), captures the low point of his life.*

Coach Brock relaxes in the dugout with shortstop Mike Henderson and pitcher Tom Van Der Meersche.

As catcher Chris Bando looks on, Coach Brock changes pitchers during the 1977 drive for the College World Series championship.

There's no doubt about Hubie Brooks' feelings after beating South Carolina 2-1 to take the 1977 College World Series.

Coach Brock and wife Pat pose with Roger and Nancy Schmuck (left) and Pat and Jan Kuehner.

think you want to put me off this morning."

About an hour into the program, he finally turned and said, "I've got a surprise. Coach Brock wants to say something to us." Then he went quickly to his chair and started praying.

I had been coaching for seventeen years and had made hundreds of talks, but it hit me as I stood up at that long table that after all those hundreds of talks, I finally had something to say.

I looked out at that audience of young athletes and saw five baseball players from my own team. I had often made fun of those five guys. I'd told them if they would quit spending so much time in church, they might be better players. There were fifty-five other athletes there as well, and I learned at that moment what it means to let the Holy Spirit guide you. He gave me the words to tell what had happened twenty-four hours before and how everything was going to be not a little different, but totally different.

Later on, I learned how those Christian ballplayers responded. Outfielder Mike Colbern told someone, "We had no idea at all coach was going to get up and speak. When he did, especially with the events that had happened the day before, it was unbelievable. We were all overjoyed that our coach had become a Christian."

Pitcher Floyd Bannister added, "Quite a few players had committed their lives to Christ, and it meant a lot to know that the guy who was going to lead us in baseball had also done so. After he accepted Christ, the biggest thing about Coach Brock was his rapport with the players. Before he'd been totally win-oriented. He still wanted to win every game, but now he cared about us, communicated with us, and understood our feelings. Before, you couldn't give him any input. Now you could."

We live in a hectic household, and with the ball games that weekend, the athletic breakfast, and visiting Bump in the hospital, Pat and I never talked again about that visit with Pastor Davidson. When I suggested that we go to church Sunday morning, she didn't act too suprised. After all, it was Easter.

After church, however, Pastor Davidson's wife stopped us. Someone had told her about my surprise remarks at the athletes' breakfast, and she wanted to know if I'd repeat them at church that night. Pat heard the conversation and wondered what it could have been that they would ask me to repeat in a church.

I hadn't planned that Saturday morning talk. I hadn't known what I was going to say until I stood up there. I'd just prayed and asked God to tell me what to say. That was the athletic world I lived in, however; speaking in church was something else.

I sat that Sunday afternoon with pencil and paper to plan what I would say, but it wouldn't come. That evening the auditorium was dark, just a spotlight illuminated the platform, and I was shaking as I moved into it. I was standing before fifteen hundred complete strangers to talk about something I didn't completely understand, and I realized my wife would also hear it for the first time.

I had brought her in on this revelation slowly. First, she caught my mood at lunch on Friday. Then she noticed some changes in my behavior. Now she would hear me explain it.

As a Christian, I was learning to be more thankful for things I had taken for granted—and that included Pat and our children, Cathi and Bucky. Again, I prayed and asked God for the right words. I told the congregation I had given my life to Jesus Christ, that he was part of me, and I planned to serve him. I didn't know what he had in mind for me, but I was terribly happy, excited, and relieved.

Pat knew then that she was living with an entirely new man.

Now that I was of a mind to listen, she told me of her own conversion eleven years before. She had gone to a lot of churches before she realized that most important was knowing Jesus Christ as a person, and she had acknowledged him as her Savior.

Suddenly, coaching was fun again. Not because we were winning. Winning was still very, very important to me, of course, and I was still living in a world where I got the credit for winning and the blame for losing. But it was no longer the central thing in my life. The new bottom line was serving the Lord. I wanted to be judged on how hard I worked to be the best Christian coach around, not on how many games we won. I became much more philosophical about the future. Maybe the Lord's plan for me was that in three weeks I would be fired. If that was the case, I was ready to accept the Lord's plan and be

91

thankful for it, as strange as that may sound.

My basic coaching tool in recent years had been intimidation. I felt I could be effective because I could motivate through fear, through being tough and mean. I never gave pep talks. I gave ultimatums. The players' reward for winning was a "parole" from my harangues. I always believed the way you became a better coach was to become a better actor. There was no way you could afford to react to a club the way you really felt. Once in a while, your natural reaction was the correct one for the situation, of course. But not very often.

In some ways, I knew, the best time to get on your players is when the team is going good, because that's when they can take it. But I couldn't seem to do it that way.

Actually, I had been drawing a blueprint for the scaffold I seemed to climb each year at Omaha in the early years of my ASU career. The pattern was clear enough: The Devils would lose early in the season. I would terrorize them into winning, then "reward" them by leaving them alone. They routinely ended the regular season with long victory strings, but by the time they got to Omaha each year, they'd been on "parole" so long they were actually out of my reach.

When our team won, it actually got away from me. I was most effective as a coach when we were in a slump. I was very good as taking back the reins during the regular season, but of course there wasn't that much time in the College World Series.

As a Christian, I found myself coaching less from

panic. I got out of the punish-first-ask-questions-later syndrome; I even asked for other people's opinions, which before had seemed like weakness to me. As a result, the players now felt less threatened and more inclined to approach me.

But the thing that changed most dramatically for me after I accepted Christ, of course, was my relationship with the players. A few weeks after Easter two of my players called me about 3:00 A.M., which was something they wouldn't have had the nerve to do before. It seemed that a former player, one of the few I'd been very close to, had moved into an apartment with a couple of other ex-players, who were both Christians. This fellow was from a Jehovah's Witness background. The Christian kids were talking to him about a personal relationship with Christ, and it was confusing him. On top of that, a girl with whom he was very much in love had told him she didn't want to see him any more.

That night he got drunk, came home, and crashed his fist through the door. His roommates weren't able to calm him down, and he went out again. They were really worried, figuring he might jump off a bridge or hurt himself somehow.

We finally found him and took him back to his room, and in the next half hour as we talked, I was closer to him than I'd ever been to an athlete. I felt God was using me to help calm him down, and I put my arm on his shoulders, practically embracing him. That was an entirely new experience for me. I never could have shown that kind of feeling for

anyone outside my family, especially a male baseball player. I would have thought something was
wrong with me, but now I felt quite comfortable.

Of course, Christians bleed when they're cut and
cry when they're hurt just like everybody else. My
first reaction to a crucial loss on the ball field is still
the totally human one: heartbreak. But now I realize
God has a plan for my life, and I can find a certain
underlying peace in the midst of disappointment.

Some changes have been harder to make than
others. I had a salty vocabulary that I used regularly
on the players as well as umpires. Then, because I
knew it was wrong, I tried to adopt new language
patterns, but you don't change a lifetime of habits
overnight.

We were about to leave town one afternoon when
Athletic Director Fred Miller stepped on the bus.

"Good luck, you guys," he hollered. "I know you
can do it."

Whereupon some wise guy at the back of the bus
yelled, "We probably could if we had decent meal
money."

That embarrassed me. Then while we were check-
ing in at the airport, the public address system announced, "Mr. Brock, please pick up a white paging
phone."

It was our assistant athletic director telling me
that some of the players who'd been staying at a
motel since school closed had done about $400 worth
of damage. With that ringing in my ears, I got on the
plane. I was sitting up front, and the team was way

in the back. Halfway through the flight, a stewardess, not knowing I was with the team, commented, "Boy, that's the rudest bunch of guys I've ever seen."

When the plane stopped in Denver, I strolled back and asked the team captain to get the players together for a little meeting. I was so angry by this time I reached back to my old vocabulary and ripped into them. I regretted it as soon as I had done it, but it was too late.

A similar outburst came one night in Oklahoma when I ran into an umpire who severely tested me. I helped to finance my education by umpiring high school games, and, while I have long since given up my mask, blue suit, whisk broom, and funny little hat, I have never given up my umpire's card. It's a good thing, too, because on this particular night the umpires needed all the help they could get.

I was uptight because our number one ranking was in jeopardy if we lost that one, and I was convinced the local umpires were giving the hometown boys an edge.

I went into the dugout on the edge of losing control and prayed, "Lord, help me!" The Lord knows when we just mouth words without meaning them in our hearts, and I clinched it by praying, "Lord, we've got to have this one!"

Two innings later, when I could take no more, I ran from the dugout to the plate and caught myself just as I stopped in front of the umpire.

"You know you're not umpiring very well." I tried to be calm.

"I'm umpiring better than your team is playing," he came back.

With that, I called him every name I've ever known and some I didn't even know I knew. Satan got behind me to prompt me, but instead of throwing Satan out, the ump threw us both out.

In a lot of ball parks you can leave through a tunnel from the dugout; no one sees you. In this one you have to walk up through the stands. I hadn't exactly captured the hearts of the Oklahoma fans, and they were delighted to accompany my exit with an assortment of remarks and gestures.

I was very much aware that I had completely fouled up. It wasn't one of those borderline cases that you can rationalize away as a slip of the tongue. No, four thousand people had witnessed this one, and I had to do something about it.

I did, of course, ask God for forgiveness, but I knew that wasn't enough. After the game I had to find that umpire and straighten things out with him. I searched for him and finally, just as we were about to board our team bus, I found him.

"Ump, ump," I called.

"That was a good call, you turkey," he yelled, "and you should have been thrown out."

"No, no! I want to apologize. That was wrong for me to talk that way. I'm a Christian and I'm sorry it happened. Will you forgive me?"

"Well, I guess so."

Obviously, he was startled. That was probably the

first time in his career a coach had apologized for anything.

I climbed on our bus feeling much better and put the incident out of my mind. Later I learned that another umpire had overheard the conversation. He was a Christian and told the story over and over. So I feel that not only did I receive forgiveness, but somehow God used the incident for good.

At the end of that season, we went down to Tucson with a chance to win the division championship and advance to the WAC playoffs. Instead, we lost all three games, including one in which we had a 9-2 lead. It was heartbreaking to lose to the Wildcats and very tough on the pride to be swept. But Pat and I went out after the game with Betty and Kemp Biddulph and consoled ourselves with the thought we had almost everybody coming back, while Arizona was losing practically everybody. Then, in the days following that series, something entirely unexpected took place.

I had always required every player to stop by and see me before he left for the summer. This year some of them commented on how much they had hated the first part of the season. Several said they had vowed never to come back to Arizona State no matter what. Most of them said they weren't exactly sure what had happened, but that the second half of the season had certainly been a lot more fun. The Christian kids, of course, knew exactly what had happened. For the first time since the early years at Mesa, or even since high school, I started to feel close to many of my players, and it was a very good feeling.

That was the only year in the last nine that a team of mine had finished lower than third nationally. But my compensation was the thrill of having those young men look me in the eye and say, "Coach, there are some things we really like about you."

The world looked bright and new again. We had nineteen of the top twenty-one players coming back, and Floyd Bannister was going to be the best ASU pitcher ever. That June I eagerly looked forward to my first full season as a Christian coach.

My Plan for God

9

WHILE I LOOKED FORWARD to the 1975 season more than I had to any season for years, it would be, I was soon to learn, a real test of my new faith. For the first time in my life, I was aware that God had a plan for me, and I was determined to follow it. Now, while the scorebook was no longer the most important book in my life, I still had a burning desire. Perhaps more than ever before I wanted to win the national championship that had eluded me since I came to ASU.

In many ways I felt I was a better coach since I had accepted Christ. In fact, if I hadn't accepted him, I couldn't have stayed in coaching. Under no circumstances could I have gone on handling the pressure by myself. So I was a better coach if for no other reason than I was a happier coach. Don't misunderstand me. I still struggled with disappointment when an athlete was injured, when I lost good players to the pros, when an umpire made a poor call. Becoming a Christian didn't solve everything, but it made it easier to accept what couldn't be solved.

I think many people live with the myth that Christianity should turn a person into a plaster saint. I learned right away that it didn't. I still lost my temper (especially at umpires), gossiped, overreacted, did foolish things. I had the same temptations everyone had, but hopefully I was making some progress as I grew in the Christian faith.

Often, after I had slipped and made a cutting remark to my wife or snapped at a coach or intimidated a player, I had a recurring fantasy. I imagined myself in a hassle-free world, sitting in a rocking chair on a front porch, reading the Bible. People would stop to say loving things, and peace reigned around me. Quickly I learned I had to stay in the competitive world I had chosen, with all its traps and pressures and temptation. Next I realized that that's the way I wanted it—at least for the moment.

Actually, college baseball is a very clean sport. I've never heard of the NCAA putting a school on probation for a baseball violation. Anyhow, we had a new 8,000-seat stadium and often filled it, bringing in a fairly tidy sum for the athletic program.

I had never had quite the same pressure that some college football or basketball coaches have to fill stadiums, so the temptation to cheat or manipulate the rules had not been the same. I don't think I would have done those things before becoming a Christian anyhow, and I knew I wouldn't now.

The first day of practice that year, I noticed a

different atmosphere. In the past when I'd come on the field, I'd been aware of a gap between me and the players. I'd never liked it, but I thought it was necessary. I thought that's how you maintained discipline, even though it made me uncomfortable. Players would speak to me only when I spoke to them. Practices had always been very tightly organized, almost like surgical operations with everything in exact sequence and very sterile.

Now I found myself able to open up. I was much more comfortable, not nearly as tense. The players still knew that if they messed up, I might get on them, but it didn't seem to happen as often.

The change showed up first through the bond I had with the Christian players, and it seemed to spread. I was happy to be the baseball coach at Arizona State University and very excited about our prospects. I was having fun, and the team caught and took on my enthusiasm.

When a man did something wrong, I asked myself if I had explained things clearly. All coaches tell players what they do wrong, but most of us don't handle it well. We tend to think that either the guy doesn't care, or he's too dumb to learn. That might be the case sometimes, but often it's just poor communication.

Coaches also forget how hard it is to understand what someone is explaining when you're emotionally charged up. The most important thing in a player's life may be playing baseball for ASU. It's what he wants to do more than anything in the world, and I'm the one who controls that hope. No wonder he's easily confused when I'm talking to him. As a Christian, it was a lot easier for me not to assume it was his fault. Maybe, just maybe, it was mine.

I found also that I couldn't always run a successful ball club with a book of exacting rules. When I recognized my players as individuals, I not only made exceptions to those previously sacrosanct decrees of mine, but I felt I could have a different set of rules for each player.

I also felt a greater sense of coaching freedom. I was free to function as a head coach in a staff situation rather than being pinned down by any one phase of the game (which was usually pitching). Two years before, I had hired twenty-six-year-old Pat Kuehner from the Southern Cal baseball staff. Kuehner, a three-sport star at La Serna High School in Whittier, California, had gone to USC on an academic scholarship. He earned all-conference honors in baseball, and his ninth-inning triple in the final game of the 1968 College World Series against Southern Illinois had given the Trojans the title. He signed with the Washington Senators and got as high as the Eastern League. While at Burlington, North Carolina, in 1970, he went six-for-six, scored six runs, and drove in ten in one game to set a Carolina League record. He went back to USC to complete work on his master's in physical education, then stayed on as USC's first full-time baseball assistant coach. The Trojans won

two more NCAA titles during his stint as Rod Dedeaux's right-hand man.

It was obvious from the beginning that Pat was
an excellent recruiter, and he got even more effective
as a hitting instructor as time went on. In fact, the
first year, the team set an NCAA record with a .333
batting average. Even with all our troubles in 1974,
we had a very respectable .291 team batting average.

To help with the pitching in 1975, I promoted one
of my old Mesa College All-Americans, Roger
Schmuck, from jayvee status. In a way, it seemed an
odd choice, because as a player Roger had never been
much help to pitchers, either under me at Mesa or
under Winkles at ASU. Schmuck blasted away at a
.381 career clip while earning All-America honors
as a Sun Devil, and nobody before or since ever had a
year quite like the one he put together in 1971—a .434
average, twelve home runs, eighty runs batted in,
and an NCAA record forty-five-game hitting streak.
During the streak, Schmuck hit .477, with ten home
runs and sixty-six RBIs, and had a slugging percentage of .839. At least he should be able to tell the
pitchers what they were doing wrong.

Actually, Roger had been a pitcher in high school,
and he'd done a little pitching for me at Mesa. I think
he also pitched some in pro ball. He had a tremendous rapport with the players and added a dimen-
sion that might not have been there before. He was
very strong on fundamentals, and, since he'd learned
them from me, we thought the same way. He had

the ability to analyze pitching faults and the patience to work on those faults until there was real improvement.

This was the same club from the year before, coming of age. People who had been good prospects the year before were now good college players, coming off fine summers in nonpro baseball. Still, forgetting everything else that had happened, this had after all been a 39-24 ball club the year before. We knew it would be better, but how much better?

It was obvious that in Floyd Bannister we had a super ace for the next two years. He was the epitome of everything we tried to teach about pitching, and he was unbelievably dedicated. In fact, he's probably the most dedicated player I ever had—but we almost never had him.

Floyd Franklin Bannister, the star southpaw who would later find fame and fortune with the Houston Astros, came to Arizona State more by accident than design. In fact, he wasn't even on my recruiting list, and if Bill Schaeffer, Frank Bradley, and Frank Papasedero hadn't interfered, Bannister probably would have gone to the University of Arizona.

In July of 1974 we lost a top pitching prospect to the pros. In fact, we lost several over a two-week span, and we really needed a pitcher, preferably a lefthander. Along about this time, I got a call from Bill Schaeffer (of Schaeffer & Smith Insurance, which sponsors our postgame radio shows). He told me that this friend of his (Bradley) had told him that this kid (Bannister) from Seattle was coming down to visit our campus, and that he was a great one. I'd never heard the name before, but I got out my draft list, and sure enough, there it was—"Oakland (3rd round), Floyd Bannister."

I called Bradley to learn that Bannister had played summer ball for Papasedero in Seattle and that Floyd was playing for him now. So I called Papasedero, who told me my information was right except for one thing—Bannister was going to Tucson to visit the University of Arizona campus.

Right away the bristles went up my neck, and, with trembling fingers, I dialed Floyd. He told me he planned to fly down to Tucson at his own expense, and I told him I had a much better idea. Why didn't I just offer him a full scholarship right now over the phone and also pay his expenses for a trip down to our campus? He said, gee, he didn't know. Maybe he'd better check with Coach Kindall. So I told him I certainly saw no need for that at all. He thought it over some and finally said he'd come.

It must have been 120 in the shade the day he came in. He was what I call a very high-class young man, courteous, well-dressed, and he had a perfect build for a pitcher. He seemed terribly interested in getting an education, and he was probably recruited more by our engineering technology department than anything else. He was on campus about six hours and signed a letter of intent when he got back home. Now I only had to worry about two things the rest of the summer: Would he turn pro . . . and could he pitch?

The answers turned out to be "no," and "you better

107

believe it." Bannister had pitched Seattle's Kennedy High School to the 1973 state championship, and he'd been the Most Valuable Player in the Babe Ruth World Series that year. His prep career record was 31-3, and his earned run average was under 1.00. His senior year, he'd gone 16-0, with an ERA of 0.00 (he gave up a run but it was unearned). Oakland made no serious effort to sign him (offering only $8,000), and Floyd showed up in Tempe right on schedule in the fall of '74.

I was standing out on the mound at Sun Devil Field, and some guy was throwing in the bullpen. I wasn't sure who it was, but even from that distance, I could see he threw very smoothly and had great leverage. It was Bannister, and when I went down to watch him throw, I got very excited. The only problem was he didn't have a curveball. As hard as he threw, he hadn't needed one in high school. It was just a matter of making a few changes in his form, because he was already very close to everything we tried to teach our pitchers. While he was learning that curveball, he was hittable—hittable, perhaps, but not beatable.

Floyd appeared in fifteen games with the varsity his freshman season and wound up with a 4-0 record. That summer he pitched the Fairbanks, Alaska, Goldpanners to the national nonpro championship, and the pros couldn't touch him until the end of his junior year. He seemed like a perfect player.

There were other reasons to feel good about the team's chances that fall, too, for example, Greg

Cochran. Greg was a good Christian guy who'd had three agonizing years of arm problems. I always felt he had a great deal of potential, but he'd never really had a chance to do much pitching. We put him through the Jon Cole rehabilitation program, working with weights and doing other exercises, and now it seemed as though in his senior year his arm was going to be all right.

Then there was Jerry Maddox, a two-time All-American from Cerritos (California) Junior College, who had been drafted four times (three by Kansas City; once by Minnesota). In his last four seasons before coming to ASU, he had hit under .400 only once; his first year, he'd hit .446. Maddox had started very slowly as ASU's regular third baseman in 1974, and, even with a late flurry, wound up hitting only .287. He'd been shifted to shortstop now, and like so many others on the team, seemed ready to bloom.

Clay Westlake, the big first baseman, had hit .382 for the Devils as a freshman but fallen off seventy-three points in 1974. I was reasonably sure Clay would bounce back strongly.

Ken Landreaux had hit only .243 as a freshman, but he had just had a great summer. He'd been drafted very low, but it was obvious by that time that that had been a big mistake. Ken was probably our most complete player. You see a lot of one-tool players, but he was a three-tool man—hit, run, field.

So the Sun Devils were clearly loaded, but the big question on my mind was how would I stand up under pressure? It was almost as though I was start-

109

ing my career over again, and I had many of the doubts and questions that always come with a new job. I didn't worry about it the way I used to, but I certainly had some doubts.

At times I was concerned about that favorite tool of mine, intimidation, having been taken away. Would discipline suffer? Would I be able to motivate the club without threatening? And how would I deal with the popular misconception that a Christian has to have the doormat syndrome, that he wants to be walked on? The answers to all these questions began to fall in place fairly early in the season. It's not easy to change coaching styles in mid-career, but by the end of the first month, I felt I'd made the transition.

The season itself was everything I thought it might be. Maddox set an NCAA record with twenty home runs, missed Schmuck's school slugging record of .740 by ten percentage points, came within one RBI of Al Bannister's record of ninety, and won the Lefty Gomez Plate as outstanding amateur player of the year. Floyd Bannister was 15-4 with an ERA of 1.66 and fell only twelve shy of Gary Gentry's national strikeout mark of 229. He had single-game highs of eighteen, seventeen, and fifteen (in the College World Series), his 217 strikeouts led the nation, and he was a first-team All-American. Cochran was 14-0 in the regular season as he set a career mark for consecutive victories (eighteen). Landreaux hit sixteen home runs, drove in seventy-seven runs, and set a school record for runs scored (eighty-four). Westlake set a school doubles record (twenty-six) ... and on it

110

went. Even the player shifts I made (Garry Allenson from catcher to third; Tommy Sain from the outfield to second) worked out perfectly.

We got off to a good start, and though we'd done that before, this time it was really exciting. The players seemed to improve at a rate I'd never seen before. We were all pulling together. We won our first sixteen conference games, including the first four against Arizona. They won the last two, but we had already clinched the division championship. Brigham Young University gave us no problems in the WAC playoffs, and although we lost once in the double-elimination regional, we took that championship as well. We won the final game against Washington State and took a 58-11 record to the World Series in Omaha.

In the middle of the season, things were going so well I remember thinking what a wonderful year it was. We had no discipline problems at all, nor personnel problems. God's plan for me, I thought, was becoming fairly obvious. For thirty-seven years I'd lived by *my* plan. Suddenly, I was living by God's plan. I was saying, "Hey, whatever he wants me to do, I'll do," hoping it wouldn't be missionary work in Africa. At the same time, however, I had a third plan going, sort of my plan for God. Anything that *I* figured was good for God's plan, I expected him to include.

When we looked at the competition in Omaha, it seemed very average, and I felt good about our chances. I had real confidence. God's plan for me as a new

111

Christian coach was to win the national championship. What else could it be? Think of the places I could witness for him. I thought to myself, "I'll give Jesus at least part of the credit. I'll work his name in there every time I have a chance."

There was no hint of disaster. Bannister survived a shaky start and went on to register fifteen strikeouts in a 5-3 win over Cal Fullerton. In the second game, a sensational relief stint by freshman Tom Van Der Meersche (one hit in the final 4-2/3 innings) keyed a 5-2 victory over powerful Texas. Bannister was rested and ready for South Carolina, but the Gamecocks climbed all over him for four runs in the fourth inning and won, 6-3.

It was the only time all year he was really hit hard, and now I had to make a big decision as we got ready for Oklahoma, a team for which I had great respect. I could have come back with Cochran, of course, but the fact was we'd have to get a win somewhere along the line from somebody other than our aces to win the championship. So, in one of the guttier moves in college baseball, I started John Poloni, a lefthander who hadn't pitched in a month. We were running the risk of getting eliminated right there, but if we won, we'd be in great shape.

I'm not sure whether I would have had the guts to do it before or not, even though we had some percentages working for us. For one thing, Oklahoma had six lefthander hitters. They also generated a lot of their offense from a great running game, and Poloni had one of the best moves to first base I'd ever seen.

Poloni walked one, struck out eight, and allowed only two Sooners as far as second base as he fashioned a four-hit shutout. At that, he was no better than he had to be, because Arizona State didn't score until the eleventh inning, when Landreaux outlegged an infield roller, moved to second on a sacrifice, and came home on Bob Pate's single. The Devils had themselves a reprieve and a rematch with South Carolina.

All the Gamecocks had left was their number three pitcher, who hadn't pitched at all in the World Series. We had Cochran, who was 18-0 lifetime as a college pitcher, and then we could come back with Bannister the next night. Well, their man pitched much better against us than he should have, and it was scoreless after 7½ innings. It didn't seem to matter, however, because Cochran was pitching the best game of his career. In the bottom of the eighth, Pate singled and Maddox tripled, and if anything was ever obvious, it was that we were going to win. How could we miss. We've even got a Christian pitcher out there.

Their first man in the ninth got on on a drag bunt. The second guy sacrificed as they went for the tie. The next man hit a bouncer to third base, but it bounced a little higher than we hoped, glanced off the top of our five-foot, eight-inch third baseman's glove, and rolled into the left-field corner. That made it 1-1 with a man on second. They scored three more times; we went quietly in our ninth; and I was zero-for-three at Omaha.

I was standing in front of the dugout, and I just

couldn't believe it was happening. Usually, I'm the eternal pessimist and always coach from the standpoint that if anything can go wrong, it will. This time, however, I had had tremendous confidence that we were going to win the national title. The third time in Omaha was going to be the charm. It was all part of a plan. The year had gone so well; it was unbelievable it could end like this.

I was disillusioned and brokenhearted, but I knew I had to get upstairs to the press box. It would be in very bad taste not to show up for the postgame show. Since the crowd was coming down and I was going up, it took me quite a while to get to the press box, and I'm sure I was crying. About halfway up there, it finally hit me. All this stuff about winning the national championship had been *my* plan for God, not God's plan for me.

The interlocutor on the postgame show was Doug Gerlach, whose modest title as assistant sports information director severely understated his actual skills. He already had two degrees, was on his way to law school, handled all the baseball publicity at ASU, and also did play-by-play and color commentary on the Sun Devil network.

Doug does a lot of things well, but better than anything else is the way he handles defeats on the postgame show. He only makes me mad when we win. I told the people that I was heartbroken, but that I accepted what had happened as part of God's plan. Later I took a great deal of criticism for that. Some people thought I was saying that winning wasn't very important to me. Others said, "That Brock is really something. One year he blames Omaha on bad breaks, and another year it's bad umpiring. Now he's blaming God."

I did care very much, of course, and it certainly wasn't God's fault. But that criticism would keep until I got home. The next few hours I experienced the greatest thrill I had had since becoming a Christian.

In the past when we'd lost at Omaha, and the guys came to say good-bye, it was a totally down situation, a terrible time. The good-byes hurt almost as much as the loss. Usually after that last loss I could see everybody in about forty-five minutes and say everything necessary. It was almost like talking to someone at a funeral. "He was such a good man . . . a shame he had to die," etc.

This time it took almost four hours, and it was definitely up. The kids felt sorry they had lost, sorry for themselves, for the team, and for the school. But for the first time they also felt sorry for the coach. There was a bond there; we'd become like a family. It hadn't been just a matter of me giving orders and calling the shots. We'd become friends.

I don't remember the exact words any player spoke, but at 3:30 A.M., when Pat and I went out to see if we could find an open restaurant, I was feeling great and actually looking forward to 1976. The whole year had been so positive, in spite of the final disappointment, I felt only fatigue and a deep sense of peace.

The Spirit of '76

10

WE HAD SOME HOLES TO FILL to start the campaign of 1976. But again, the players had showed tremendous improvement during the summer in nonpro ball, and I began to tell myself this could really be a good one.

Pitching was pretty thin behind Floyd Bannister, but the potential was there for one of the best hitting teams ASU had ever had. No school had ever had two players chosen in the first round of the pro draft before, but it became obvious that Bannister and Ken Landreaux were going to be high selections. As it turned out, both were chosen in the first round (Bannister first and Landreaux fifth), and outfielder Mike Colbern went high in the second round. Also included in our returning group were Clay Westlake, Gary Allenson, Ken Phelps, and Bob Pate. We had eleven regulars back from last year's team that had come so close to winning it all.

Rick Peters, a switch-hitter who could really run, was developing into a first-class infielder. At third base, we had a big guy named Brandt Humphry, who'd led the jayvee team the year before. My assistant coach Pat Kuehner had always liked Humphry, but I was only lukewarm. It turned out Pat was right, and Humphry had a fine year.

Then we had two super freshman prospects. There was no question from the minute he stepped on the campus that Bobby Horner from Apollo High School in Glendale was going to be a tremendous hitter. We felt he would help us immediately, and of course he eventually became a first-team All-American. Then we had a guy from Concordia, California, named Mitch Dean, who had the potential to be as good a relief pitcher as we'd had in quite a while.

I was coming off a pretty good summer myself. Criticism showed up pretty regularly in the letters to the editor of the morning paper, some questioning my coaching and some the sincerity of my Christian witnessing. But I could handle that now. I was much more comfortable with my faith and had a better idea of how to use it more effectively. I knew I still had a lot to learn and would never reach perfection, but on the other hand, I was no longer a "rookie."

We started a once-a-week Bible study session in our house. At first, we weren't quite sure whether it should be an in-depth study of the Bible, a time to share our faith with other athletes, or what. It turned out to be an informal, loosely structured time of sharing what each person had learned from the Bible. The guys actually conducted the meetings, although sometimes I took a few minutes to make some spiritual point that related to an event of the past week.

Meetings were strictly volunteer. In fact, I refused to talk to the whole team about it. Before each season, now, I'll just introduce one of the players who's involved and say something such as "Mike has asked for some time to say something to the team." Then Mike will tell about the weekly meetings.

At that point, I emphasize that attendance is by no means mandatory and in no way affects a player's chances with the team. Then, I might joke that Mike is going to be the first speaker, so each person will have to decide for himself whether or not the food we serve will be worth having to listen to him.

One year, of the nine players who were the most faithful attenders of the weekly meetings, six didn't make the trip to Omaha. I hadn't even been aware of it, but when we got to the hotel, one of the players said, "Hey, coach, we can't have a Bible study because there are only three of us here." I try to base all my recruiting or travel squad decisions entirely on who can help the team the most.

Our recruiting in 1976 had slumped somewhat as the effects of the NCAA's thirteen-scholarship ceiling (down from twenty-eight) started showing up. I felt badly about that, because it was depriving a lot of young men of a chance to get a college education.

But as far as the team was concerned, we couldn't complain, because we had gotten Horner and Dean. All in all, it had been a good summer.

Roger Schmuck had been lured over to Mesa College as assistant baseball coach, and Gary Pullins, who had played Legion ball for me, was the replacement. Gary, on leave from his coaching job at Utah Tech to complete his doctorate in physiology at ASU, wanted some major-college coaching experience, so it worked out well. Pullins had spent four years in the Dodger organization as a player and coach and would later become the head baseball coach at Brigham Young University.

Fall ball really didn't go too well, and I wasn't quite sure why. The intensity seemed much lower than it had been the previous fall. I didn't get too excited about it, though. I guess perhaps I figured the guys were veterans now, and fall ball just wasn't that big a deal to them. I still felt we had a chance for a good year.

We got off to a slow start in the spring. We were winning, but we were having to scramble against teams we should have beaten easily. The players seemed to be working hard, but they had no killer instinct, and they were losing a little too gracefully to suit me. It was almost like they were saying, "Hey, it's a long season, so a loss now and then is no big deal." But I certainly wasn't saying that, and as the conference season drew closer, I grew more and more concerned.

I must admit that after a couple of our early season

losses, I was tempted to revert back to the old Jim Brock, to scream, threaten, and intimidate. I wanted to get those guys out there on that left-field line and give them something they'd understand. I was frustrated, and my faith was tested, but I was determined to have patience.

I tried every other tactic in my repertoire—team meetings, gentle persuasion, one-on-one talks, everything. Nothing seemed to work.

Then came an almost classic test of faith. Things had, after all, gone rather smoothly up to now since I had accepted Christ. There had been occasional setbacks, of course, but never any motivational problems, never any need for the whip. Now I realized the whip needed cracking. And, through a strange quirk of fate, La Verne College was back in town.

We had a three o'clock game and a seven o'clock game. It so happens there was a young man, never one of my personal favorites, who had pitched in our jayvee program without much success. Somehow, he had talked his way into La Verne, and there he was pitching against us in the three o'clock game. He pitched a pretty good game and beat us by about five runs.

Needless to say, I was a little upset. We had a couple of hours between games with no place to go and nothing really to do, and even the nicest of coaches might have gone to distance running in that situation.

I was sure we had to run—no doubt in my mind about that. But at the same time, I knew my feeling about running was very different than it had been before. Before, my feeling had always been one of anger and frustration, a chance to get even, intimidation. Now, it seemed important to me that the players understand that, while they probably didn't want to run, we had tried a lot of other things, and maybe this was what we needed right now. There was another big difference, too. I didn't want to embarrass them. In the past, I'd never really cared who knew what was going on when I went to the whip. I would take them out in the outfield to run, even though the other team was out there eating between-game sack lunches. If there was a little embarrassment to go with the torture, well, so much the better. But no more.

I called the team together in the dugout and told them to walk slowly over to the track, and that I would meet them there because we needed to talk. I waited a few minutes and followed them. Calmly I told them that at one time in my career, I would have enjoyed this type of activity. But not now. I said I wished I was a better coach so that I wouldn't have to resort to this, but obviously I was not, so this is what we had left. It was sort of the old this-is-gonna-hurt-me-more-than-it-hurts-you spiel kids hear before a spanking.

I made a conscious effort to avoid any inferences of intimidation. I did not call them any names; I made no threats that if this didn't work I would do something worse. I said we were going to run for a while, and that we were going to run hard, and after they

124

finished, I wanted them to have a team meeting behind closed doors without me. Then we proceeded to run, and run, and run, and run.

I hoped that I had "kept the faith" and yet demonstrated that *Christian* and *Milquetoast* are not interchangeable labels.

We won twenty-nine of our next thirty-one games. Once again La Verne had brought us to a turning point.

A few weeks later, we had an important road trip. We opened with back-to-back losses to Texas but came back to win a doubleheader. The next night, we were trailing 9-0 in the eighth inning at Tulsa. Landreaux got hit by a pitch. He had skinny little arms anyway, and we were afraid he'd broken one. You could actually see the seam marks from the ball. It took quite a while to ice the arm down, and the umpire seemed to share our concern. But when we finally got Ken started in the direction of first base, the ump said, "Hey, where's he going? That was a foul ball."

I lost my composure. I didn't say anything profane, but maybe I did bump him a little bit. Anyway, I was invited to leave the premises.

Later in the inning, Pat Kuehner got thrown out too. He had never been thrown out of a game before, and since he was smarter than I was anyhow, he refused to go. The umpires finally said, "Aw, who cares? Let him stay." We proceeded to score thirteen runs and win the ball game. It was an awesome display (the hitting, that is, not the coaching).

Anyway, we beat Tulsa easily the next night, and zipped on down to Norman and beat Oklahoma twice—once on a two-out, two-strike home run by Westlake. Then we went on to Riverside and demolished the opposition.

It was perhaps the most impressive regular-season road performance in ASU history. The Devils were really rolling. In fact, we rolled over archenemy Arizona six straight times en route to the WAC Southern Division championship. In the past, this would have put the Wildcats out of it. But this time, because of a change in NCAA playoff procedures the preceding season, it merely set the stage for the Devils to play Butch Cassidy to Arizona's posse. (In the Butch Cassidy epic, the posse chased, and chased, and chased, until finally Butch said, "Well, we finally got rid of 'em." About two hundred feet further downreel, here would come the posse again. The posse's reappearance became a recurring nightmare to Butch.)

Prior to 1975, participation in the NCAA playoffs had been limited to conference champions and at-large teams. Beginning that year, outstanding conference runners-up were eligible for invitation, with the provision that they be assigned to playoff berths outside their own districts. Arizona was indeed an outstanding conference runnerup. The Cats had almost as much power as the Devils, and one outstanding pitcher in Steve Powers. Our 6-0 regular-season sweep was a bit misleading, with the Devils staging barely believable comebacks several times.

126

In the back of my mind, I always felt that if we ever had to send anybody but Bannister against Powers, we would be in big trouble. That kid was a real battler.

The Devils swept through the Rocky Mountain Regional as expected, and now it was back to Heartbreak City again.

I felt pretty good. I didn't see how it was possible to put together a college team that could hit the ball any better. But in my mind, we weren't quite as good as everybody seemed to think. We had defensive lapses, our number two pitcher Don Hanna had an earned run average of nearly four, and even Bannister was not pitching as well as he should have been. He'd had a great season, but towards the end of it, all the ink he'd been getting, all the agents, and all the pressure made it tough for him to relax.

But I was confident. We were number one in the nation and this time there was no question about what we'd do in Omaha.

Look out, Butch. Here comes that posse again! Yup. You guessed it. ASU's first-round opponent was Arizona. The Wildcats had emerged as district champions. This was the first time two schools from the same conference had ever appeared in the College World Series, and the head-on collision between the two WAC powerhouses drew the largest crowd in CWS history.

Arizona led 5-2 entering in the ninth inning, and Powers had been controlling our hitters throughout the game. With two outs and Humphry on second and Horner on first, he got two strikes on Rick Peters. Peters was just protecting the plate and slapped a single to score Humphry. Ken Landreaux followed with another single to score Horner.

In a dumb move on my part, I had put in a pinch runner for Clay Westlake earlier. So now, with the tying run on second and two out, little-used Gary Rajsich was up. Gary came through with a big single to left to score Peters from second. We'd tied it 5-5, and the game went into extra innings.

In the top of the tenth, Mike Colbern reached first base on an error, and Humphry muscled a towering homer to put us on top 7-5.

Three outs away from an opening round victory. But here came the posse again. Arizona scored one run. Another runner reached second base. With two outs and the winning run at the plate, Bannister hung on to retire the last man, and the Devils survived with a 7-6 win.

Next, we beat Washington State 9-3 on some great relief work by Dean.

And then came the pitching duel of the series— Bannister, already baseball's number one draft pick and winner of the Gomez Plate (baseball's version of the Heisman Trophy) and the *Sporting News* Player .of the Year award, against Bob Owchinko of Eastern Michigan, the nation's number three draft pick.

It was one of the best pitching duels in Series history. Owchinko was a lefthander, and we had been eating up lefthanders all year. We loaded the bases with nobody out in the first inning, but had to settle for one run. Not just for the inning, for the game. Owchinko just kept getting tougher and tougher. Bannister allowed only six hits and struck out eleven, but we lost it, 2-1.

But I knew we'd still have a chance at the title if pitcher Tom Van Der Meersche could get us by Maine. Tom won 7-0 on a five-hitter.

Oh no, Butch. Not again.

Yup. There came that posse again.

Arizona had been scrambling back through the losers' bracket, obviously playing well and not folding up after the opening loss to us. So now we were going to have to beat them for the eighth time, and in the match-up I've been fearing all year—Powers against somebody besides Bannister.

But we got a break. It rained! I felt better knowing Bannister would be able to pitch again with two days' rest.

Floyd was exhausted, however. The pressures and hullabaloo that surrounded him all year finally took their toll. He felt he couldn't pitch with only two days' rest. I had to start someone else and hope Bannister would get a chance the next night of the finals.

Unfortunately, this was not ascertained until about an hour before game time, and the letdown among the players was obvious. We had a team meeting to try and turn things around. I told the kids, "Hey, we know we can beat Arizona. We've been doing it all year long." I don't think any of us really believed it.

I went with our number two man, Hanna, but he was hit early, often, and hard. Dean pitched well in relief, but by the time I got him in there, it was 4-0. Powers had been waiting for this moment for three years. When he'd been a sophomore, we'd hit him hard because he used to try and throw the ball past us, but now he had a slider that he spotted very well. He shut us out until the ninth, when we picked up a run on a wild pitch, and they won with surprising ease, 5-1.

I was now 0-4 in College World Series attempts. Ironically, for the second straight year, we had been eliminated by a team coached by a brother in Christ. Both Bobby Richardson of South Carolina (the ex-Yankee star), and Arizona's Jerry Kindall were very outspoken Christian coaches.

Arizona came back the next night to easily beat Eastern Michigan for the championship, and jubilant Wildcat fans purchased billboards in the Valley proclaiming: "ARIZONA 5, ASU 1 . . . Congratulations National Champion Wildcats!"

That game had to be the bitterest pill of my career to swallow, and as I sat in the dugout and watched Powers put us down, I started to think that perhaps God was trying to tell me something. I'd been spending more and more of my free time in evangelism recently, and perhaps the events of the past few days were an indication that I should move in that direction. Many of the critics back home would second that motion. I found myself thinking that if after five years, and a team with offensive power like this one, and a super pitcher like Bannister, I still hadn't been able to win at Omaha, I'd never be able to. And if I couldn't win at Omaha, I couldn't be a success at Arizona State.

Again, Doug Gerlach did an excellent job of handling the postgame show. It was a fairly short interview, and I didn't say much. I just wanted to get it over with.

The farewell to the players was certainly not what it had been the year before. It was a terribly down situation, the kind of thing that just shouldn't have happened. There seem to be no rhyme or reason for the loss. I remember thinking it was like what had happened to my brother Bill. He was a deep-sea mine disposal diver who went all through World War II without a scratch. A couple of weeks after the war was over, he went into a restaurant in Washington, D.C. Two guys were fighting; one tried to knife the other and missed. The knife hit Billy in the jugular and killed him.

One of the things that had made the previous year's loss easier to take had been the knowledge that we had a great club coming back. We could say to ourselves, "We missed, but wait until next year." But now, next year? The superstars would be gone, and in the back of my mind I thought maybe I would be, too. The paranoia was returning.

Even Christ didn't seem to be able to help much in the next few days. My self-pity was apparently strong enough to brush away even his helping hand. I came back to the Valley to face a flood of criticism.

I had considered calling Pastor Davidson after the game Friday night, but it was late, and I decided against it. However, when we got back to Tempe the next afternoon, there was a note in the mailbox saying he'd like to see me. He seldom gives up the pulpit on Sunday morning, but he asked me if I would preach a sermon at all three services the following week on how to handle disappointment as a Christian. I said I would try.

First, however (although I didn't feel much like it now) I had to appear at a coaching clinic at Mesa College in Grand Junction. So Pat and I and Bucky started for Colorado, a long day's drive—and much, much longer if the driver is wallowing in self-pity. It was a terrible trip.

I told Pat that God had obviously closed the baseball door for me, that he wanted me to do something else, and that I was going to be fired any day. Pat had never bought the idea of me getting out of coaching, and the mere mention of it had always been enough to start a raging argument. In fact, it still is. So there were constant arguments for fourteen hours.

When we got there, there was sleet and snow and the clinic had been cancelled, more because of lack of interest than the weather, however. They did give us a cabin, but we couldn't get the heater to work, so we started right back to Arizona. What was supposed to have been a chance to get away from all the pressures at Omaha had turned into a nightmare. And as I drove along, I started to feel another pressure. In a very short time, I was going to have to stand up in front of fifteen hundred people at eight-fifteen, nine-thirty, and eleven o'clock on Sunday morning and say something. It forced me to set aside my self-pity and say, "I've got to make this dumb speech about how to handle despair, even though I'm doing such a poor job of it. I better get to work."

I had my Bible along, but I stopped in a bookstore and bought a Bible concordance. I turned to *Despair* and went to work on my sermon. I started finding comfort almost immediately in the Bible passages indicated, and by the time I got up to speak at the first service, I was feeling much better.

As I spoke to those people on Sunday, I sensed many of them thinking, "Poor Jim had a terrible disappointment, but he's handling it well." Little did they know.

During the sermon, I quoted some of the letters to the editor that troubled me the week after Omaha.

"Jim Brock," wrote one fan, "has always been able to get a team to Omaha. Perhaps it is time we got a coach who is able to win once he gets there."

Another commented, "The generosity with which this year's College World Series was surrendered must be attributed to inferior coaching."

Still another, "What's Brock's excuse this time? God's will? The odds? The CWS scheduling?"

Then I quoted some Scripture passages that comforted me, beginning with 2 Corinthians 1:3-4. It reads, "What a wonderful God we have—he is the Father of our Lord Jesus Christ, the source of every mercy, and the one who so wonderfully comforts and

133

strengthens us in our hardships and trials."

And 1 Corinthians 9:25—"An athlete goes to all this trouble just to win a blue ribbon or a silver cup, but we do it for a heavenly reward that never disappears."

And Matthew 6:34—"So don't be anxious about tomorrow. God will take care of your tomorrow too. Live one day at a time."

Working on that sermon and delivering it to all those people was the best treatment for Omaha-itis. Afterwards I was able to cope with the disappointment pretty easily.

Next, I returned to the business at hand—recruiting. We were looking at two promising kids. Jamie Allen of Yakima, Washington, was the top high-school infielder in the country and had been picked by Minnesota in the first round of the draft. Tom Hawk, a hard-throwing six-foot, five-inch pitcher from Kettering, Ohio, was just as good a prospect. We knew Allen had been offered a lot of money by the Twins. And even if he didn't take it, the grapevine had it he was heading for USC anyway and was just paying us a courtesy visit. Pat Kuehner thought we had a chance, but admitted USC was pulling out all the stops.

Well, I never had more rapport with a kid early in a recruiting experience than I had with Allen. After we visited, Pat came by to take him around the campus. They were to drop by my house in a couple of hours. Pat asked Jamie if anything about going to college in general or to ASU in particular bothered him. It

134

turned out there was. Three months earlier, at an Athletes in Action assembly at his high school, he had received Jesus Christ as his Savior. Now he wanted to know how that would go over in college. Would the other guys make fun of him? What would the coach think? So when Jamie and I got together again, it was not as coach-recruit, but as two Christian brothers. As for Hawk, his questionnaire indicated he was very active in the Fellowship of Christian Athletes. He, too, was interested in playing on a team with other Christians and with a Christian coach.

Eventually both signed up to attend Arizona State—two of the finest athletes we've recruited.

The fact that I'm a Christian does help sometimes in dealing with certain athletes. But it also obligates me to be concerned about the player's self-interest. This has some tough implications in the classic conflict-of-interest situation when one of my players is being offered big money to turn pro.

Major-league baseball teams can draft a college player after his junior year. It's up to the player to decide whether he wants to return for his senior year or turn pro.

On one hand, it's clearly not in the best interest of the school to lose one of its stars, but on the other hand, it may very well be in the best interest of the player. As a Christian coach, I am committed to considering both sides.

Floyd Bannister's situation was a case in point. After being named College Player of the Year, Floyd still had a year of eligibility remaining. However, as the number one draft pick in the country, it seemed unlikely he'd back at Arizona State University the following season.

After being out of town for about a month, I was surprised to learn negotiations between Floyd and the Houston Astros had broken down. So I called Astro scout John Miller and invited him to lunch. I told him I should really be pulling for Floyd to come back to school, but that I believed it was in his best interest to sign now. There certainly wasn't any way he could be drafted any higher. I said I understood Houston was willing to pay Floyd $100,000, and John replied that was correct.

That afternoon, Floyd came by the house to pick up some stuff he had stored in our garage. I said, "Floyd, I'm really surprised you're not in the big leagues already." He replied that things with Houston were a real mess. I told him I understood he was willing to sign for $100,000, and he said yes, that's what he wanted.

Back I went (thinking this was a funny way to run a railroad) to Miller with word that Bannister was willing to sign for what the Astros were willing to offer. Three days later, the star lefthander did sign, had a great half-season in the minors, and went up to Houston the next season.

Becoming a Christian hasn't diminished my desire to win, but it has put it in perspective. Even though it would be easier to win with Bannister, I recognized that his career, his life, and his future were more important than a few games next season.

The Rising
of the Sun Devils

11

I'VE BEEN AROUND THE VALLEY all my life, and
I've never seen an ASU season begin quite like 1977.
A new ingredient appeared on the Arizona State
baseball scene: apathy. For the first time in the
Brock era, the natives weren't restless. In fact, they
weren't even awake. .

The start of the baseball season is always a big
deal in Tempe. But this year, even the anti-Brock
letters to the editor didn't materialize. Apparently
folks figured that if all those great names from the
year before hadn't won the national championship,
this no-name bunch certainly wasn't going to. For
the first time in my five years at ASU, sportswriters
weren't even picking us to win the WAC title.

Each year, we normally staged an intrasquad game
in which reporters from the two Phoenix papers
each coached a team, and I wrote up the game for

each Phoenix paper. The 1977 game was canceled for lack of interest by the reporters.

And, to tell the truth, even I didn't have the guts to mention "national championship" in my fall talk. In the past, I'd always said, "We know what our goal is. We've got the material here, and if everybody works hard, we can win it all." Now, it was more like, "Hey, if we really work hard, maybe we can be mediocre."

Still, the apathy upset me. I felt we would have a very good college baseball team and the media should treat us that way.

Whatever my other problems, at least I still had the support of Dr. Fred Miller. After last season's World Series loss, I had gone in to see him and, in effect, offered to resign.

I told Fred I'd had five shots at it and hadn't won, that I could certainly understand if he wanted to make a change, and that now would be a pretty good time to do it.

Fred looked at me and said, "Take another five."

Fred was like that. He supported me not only as a coach but as a person. One of the nicest introductions I ever got was when we were at an alumni steak fry in the White Mountains. Fred had introduced most of the other coaches and then came to me.

"I'm proud to introduce this next coach," he said, "because this man has recently undergone a tremendous transformation in his personal life."

Fred was a dependable source of encouragement. Only once do I remember him being hesitant about my new Christianity.

140

About a week before the first baseball broadcast in 1975, Pastor Davidson asked me to tape a one-minute commercial for Grace Community Church, and I said, "Hey, no problem."

We made the tape, and I didn't think much more about it. Later that week, as Fred and I were on our way to a luncheon, I remembered that the radio spot was going on that night, and I really hadn't cleared it through proper channels. So I mentioned it there in the car.

He frowned and said something about hoping it didn't violate church-state separation. I could see he was concerned. It got very quiet for the next five miles as he mulled things over. I prayed silently that everything would work out the way God wanted it to and that I would have the strength to accept whatever happened without overreacting.

Suddenly, Fred laughed.

"This is unbelievable," he said. "I've spent the last few months dealing with some of our athletes who've been having disciplinary problems and even problems with the police, and here I am hassling you about doing some church work. Go right ahead, it's fine."

By the time we finally got to the luncheon (we missed a turnoff during our discussion), the whole thing had turned positive.

Yet even without pressure from the A.D., I didn't allow myself any margin for error. My work was cut out for me to build a contender out of this year's squad. If we were going to do anything, every player

141

would have to play up to his full potential, and some would have to exceed theirs. Catching was a good example of why we might have trouble. We had Randy Whistler, a freshman with a broken hand, and Chris Bando, whose older brother Sal was captain of the championship Oakland A's teams. Chris was an infielder, but, at my suggestion, he had caught about twenty games in Alaska during the summer. He'd had some success there, but it was still a little scary.

As grim as the catching was, it was super compared to the pitching. We started out with two pretty fair country relievers in Tom Van Der Meersche and Mitchell Dean. But Vandy underwent arm surgery and missed fall ball, which left Dean as our only proven pitcher. Then he suffered a severe cut on his throwing thumb in a nasty fall. They sewed it up wrong and later had to operate. He missed the first eight weeks of the season.

The only good news was that Roger Schmuck was back as our pitching coach. He went right to work developing some good arms out of what was a potentially ridiculous staff. All he had to work with was two walk-ons and a senior lefthander who had never started a game at ASU and was only recently recovered from hand surgery that almost ended his career.

One of the walk-ons was Larry Eiler, a sophomore from San Diego who was at ASU mostly because we'd given his brother a scholarship. Larry had dropped out of school for a couple of years to work for his dad. I think he probably got a little tired of working and said, "Hey, Dale's going to school, why don't I go along with him?" He had a very good arm and had thrown a little bit for us the year before (3-0, ERA 1.33). He'd also pitched a perfect game with the jayvees, with his brother catching. But we really didn't expect great things from him.

The other walk-on was Jerry Vasquez, a transfer from Scottsdale Community College who had missed almost all of his last year at Scottsdale with arm trouble and had never been a big winner even when he was healthy. But he had a good slider and a great heart.

The senior lefthander was Darrell Jackson, a Los Angeles youngster who'd been plagued by recurring back spasms. All in all, it was the unlikeliest big three you ever saw, but it carried us the first half of the season and became the nucleus of the deepest pitching staff I've ever had at ASU. In fact, the first part of the year, until Jackson's back straightened out, Eiler was our starting rotation, and Vasquez was our bullpen.

There were some familiar names around, of course, and neither Pat Kuehner nor I ever had any doubts about the club's ability to score runs. Not with Bobby Horner, Brandt Humphry, and Dave Hudgens, plus people like shortstop Mike Henderson and outfielders Rick Peters and Hubie Brooks.

I can't say enough about our captain Mike Henderson. Going into his final season, his only previous distinction had been to set a jayvee career at-bat record, which only meant it had taken him a long time to get to the varsity. Through sheer determination, Mike worked his way from mediocrity to being one of the best defensive shortstops in college baseball. Nobody could make the play in the hole like he did. I'd seen him play some the year before, and by August, I still had half a scholarship left, so I gave it to him. Why not? He was a good guy and turned out to be a tremendous team leader, physically and spiritually.

Rick Peters was another leader. We'd moved Rick to center field, and he had a great year with the glove. Our young pitchers made a lot of mistakes early, but Rick ran down quite a few of them. He also set a school record of forty-nine stolen bases.

Hudgens was a lefthanded hitter with a great stroke who had been waiting in the wings for a chance to play. He turned out to be the second leading RBI man in the NCAA. He had good power, especially when we needed it. Twice he hit grand slam home runs when we were three runs down in the late innings. Hubie Brooks in right field was our number nine hitter. But he became the best number nine hitter and RBI man in the country.

Probably one of the most amazing things was that Bando turned almost overnight into one of the best catchers in college baseball. It was uncanny that anybody who'd been catching as short a time as he had could have such a feel for handling pitchers.

But it took time for this talent to ripen and mature. In the beginning, I found myself in a strange situation. For the first time in ten years, I was coaching an underdog. Actually, I sort of enjoyed it. The fans did not seem to share the media apathy. They turned out in record numbers even for afternoon games against Brand X opposition. The team, obviously unimpressed with preseason predictions, got off to a great start. But I continued to use the nobody-thinks-you-guys-are-any-good theme as a rallying point all season—even after the Devils climbed to a number one ranking.

Great starts and all, there were still problems with pitching. The Devils were winning a lot of 11-10 games, and, with the team facing a stretch of something like thirty-two games in thirty days, I knew I had to do something, even if it was wrong.

We'd been using Jamie Allen mostly as a designated hitter against lefthanders. He'd played a little third base while Humphry was having some eye problems, but our infield was really pretty well set, and as a freshman, he certainly wasn't ready to hit the good righthanded curveball. Jamie had pitched and played the infield in high school and American Legion ball, but switching back and forth was a little hard on him. The scouts had convinced him his future was as an infielder, and I had assured him he wouldn't have to go back and forth at ASU. He had turned down an offer from the Twins, who had made him their number one draft choice.

But Jamie was the kind of kid who just died when he wasn't in there. And between our great need for pitching and his great desire to get into the game some place, well . . . one afternoon I told him to go down to the bullpen and get ready because we might use him the last couple of innings. He sprinted away, and in about three minutes word came that he was ready. He hadn't pitched in the fall or winter, and I hadn't seen him pitch since the Legion regional tournament in Yakima eight months before, but in he came.

When he got to the mound, I asked him the typical midseason question of a coach in a sophisticated major-college program: "What kind of pitches do you throw, Jamie?" He said he threw a fastball, curveball, slider, change-up, and forkball. Having seen him throw from third base, I knew the fastball had to be an awfully good weapon, so I told him not to throw anything else until I advised him otherwise. It turned out to be pretty good coaching. That fastball was later clocked at ninety-four miles per hour, which put him right up there with Tom Seaver and behind only Nolan Ryan. No matter what anybody had told him about his future, he loved it on the mound. He was the center of attention.

By now, Dean's hand was almost healed, Jackson was completely healthy, Eiler and Vasquez were throwing well, Jamie was in the bullpen, and suddenly we had five pitchers we could throw with confidence. And the hitting, which we felt might be just a shade weaker than last year's, turned out to be every bit as good. Not only that, but this bunch seemed to hit good pitchers better than any other team we'd had.

So the Devils sailed toward the conference under a full head of steam. Then we had a trip to Hawaii, and Tom Hawk's shoulder was injured on a nine-foot wave at Makapu. The damage was painful but not permanent, however, and the stay in the Islands was generally a happy one.

We came back tanned, rested, and not in any way ready to start the conference race. The New Mexico Lobos, with a new coach and new umpires, were lying in the tumbleweeds of Albuquerque waiting. The Lobos lulled us into thinking things were just like they'd always been by losing the opener, but the next day, with clutch hitting, clutch pitching, and clutch umpiring, they swept a doubleheader.

The first-game loss went into the record books as the longest game in Sun Devil history—about three weeks. And between the first and last pitch, I quit coaching at third base.

Pat Kuehner's administrative duties had increased quite a bit, and, in trying to take some of the load off him, I went back to the third-base line for the first time since my Legion days. I found I was a very colorful third-base coach who had everything but judgment.

We were losing 3-1 with one out in the final inning; Humphry was on second and Brooks on first. I put Chris Nyman in to pinch-hit, and he hit a one-bounce cannon shot off the 440-foot sign in center field that was a cinch to tie the game. Humphry, however, thinking the ball might be caught, held up, but Brooks and Nyman didn't.

147

Humphry finally realized the ball was in the next county, wheeled around third, and slipped flat on his back forty feet from home. Remembering the story of the Good Samaritan (but forgetting baseball's rules), I rushed over and pulled him up. Basically, I was afraid the other two runners were going to pass him.

About this time, I looked toward home plate, and the umpire was calling somebody out. It wasn't clear who, but in the meantime, Humphry had started toward home again. And this time he made it, all six-foot-three, 210 pounds of him, knocking the baseball and the catcher axle-over-wheelbase. Brooks was half a step behind Humphry, and mass confusion was half a step behind Brooks.

The plate umpire ruled that the game was over, that we had lost, and that he didn't want to talk about it. We'd made two outs on the play, and I couldn't figure out where. He refused to look at the rule book because he said he'd forgotten his reading glasses.

We protested the game. There had never been a protest upheld in the WAC, but this one was.

Three weeks later, with fan interest at a predictably feverish pitch, the game was resumed in Tempe before the start of the series opener there. Brooks was on third, Nyman on first, two out, and New Mexico leading, 3-2. The Lobo pitcher stepped off the mound and threw to second base. Whereupon Coach Vince Cappelli rushed out of the dugout waving a registered letter in which his umpires back home said

Brooks had missed second base. Our umpires would have none of this, the appeal was turned down, and New Mexico announced it was protesting.

Pinch hitter Mike Hildebrandt popped out to end the inning. The New Mexico umpire was right about one thing—we lost the game.

During the three week intermission, at the height of the debate, I appeared on a radio talk show and was asked why I didn't set a good Christian example for my players, admit I'd made a mistake, and forget the whole thing. I explained that I couldn't accept a two-out penalty for a one-out sin. I did, however, send Pat Kuehner back to third-base coaching.

The worst part of the whole affair was that suddenly, the posse from the last chapter was after Butch Cassidy again.

Arizona had gotten off to the worst start in its history, losing to everybody, and appeared to be dead in the water. But while we were losing to New Mexico, they started to win. Suddenly they were a real threat again. And when we lost the first game at Tucson, we found ourselves three games out of first place with eleven to play. I felt very good about the way our team was coming along but very bad about our mathematical position.

We had a team meeting before the second game at Arizona. We were facing an absolute do-or-die situation and talked at length about pride, concern for fellow-players and all the other things that coaches always talk about in such situations. The meeting probably lasted about an hour and a half. We went out, got four runs in the first inning, and never looked back.

We won those last eleven WAC games, swept BYU in Provo, and made it through the Rocky Mountain Regional without a scratch. I felt great—until I realized this meant we had to go back to Omaha again.

I knew that this club, like all the others, would be evaluated by what it did in Omaha—and so would I. I'm human enough that the criticism I heard every year when I came back home really hurt. However, I didn't think winning in Omaha would prove I was a good coach anymore than losing in Omaha proved I was a bad one. I'd never second-guessed myself in Omaha. I thought I'd coached well there, and most of the gambles I'd taken had paid off. But I had made a psychological mistake by not riding the egos on last year's team a little harder. All they had heard all year was how great they were.

But this year's team was a hungry fighter, and our players realized they would have to be at their very best to have a chance. They did a better job of using their hits than any of the others and played to their potential more consistently.

"Say the Devils do win in Omaha this time," a reporter asked me. "What will be your first thought after the last out is made? Would it be, 'Take that, fans'?"

"That might be one of my thoughts," I admitted. "But it won't be the first one. When we lost, the fans were never my first thought. The first thought was always for the guys who wouldn't be back, and I wished I'd done better by them their last time around."

Actually, the Brock bandwagon had been steadily gaining riders in the Valley in spite of four losses at Omaha. "It's time," a *Phoenix Gazette* columnist commented before the Devils headed for their fifth World Series appearance in six years, "to realize Arizona State once had a great baseball coach ... and still has one."

This year, however, disaster struck even before Omaha.

During the last practice prior to leaving for Nebraska, Nyman flipped a ball to Hudgens. It wasn't a hard throw, but Hudgens wasn't looking. He turned around just in time to get hit in the nose. We figured it would be no problem. Trainer Ray Robison sent him over to the doctor, who packed it and sent him home. In about an hour, Dave felt he had to blow his nose, and it started to bleed. We were still at practice, and he had the dugout phone number, but he didn't want to bother anybody, and tried for more than an hour to stop the bleeding himself. Finally, with the carpet getting redder by the minute, he did call for help.

He was rushed to the hospital, but he'd swallowed so much blood they were afraid to operate. They finally managed to stop the bleeding, but in a couple of hours, it started again, and his blood pressure dropped to zero. He was near death; he eventually spent twelve days in intensive care. Prognosis was for recovery, but slowly, and we left for Omaha without the nation's number two RBI man, the man who kept the opposition from pitching around our cleanup man, Bobby Horner.

The team with no margin for error had just received a major debit. Dave was a popular player, and there was a lot of concern for him on the squad. I'd never used the win-one-for-the-gipper speech much, but we did dedicate our first game at Omaha to Dave Hudgens. He didn't play in the Series, but he arrived in time to see the last two games. Ironically, Chris Nyman, the kid who tossed the ball, wound up playing first base and making the All-Tournament team.

In addition to losing their slugging first baseman, the Devils had also been stripped of their cover on the eve of the Series. We had been tiptoeing along quietly in the seven and eight spots much of the year, but in its final poll, *Collegiate Baseball* had elevated the Devils to number one.

This pressure-producing promotion was somewhat offset by the fact that many of the other biggies in college baseball—Oklahoma, Arizona, Texas, USC—were missing from this World Series. I always feel I've got a shot if I don't recognize anybody at the coaches' party the night before the Series.

We opened against Clemson. Not only were we missing Hudgens, but Brandt Humphry got a fever and was too sick to play. Jamie Allen filled in at third base.

We finally hit as well in Omaha as we normally did during the season and jumped off to a 6-0 lead in the fifth inning. Jerry Vasquez had a two-hit shutout going when Allen made an error at third. It seemed to open the gates, and before they were closed, Clemson had the go-ahead runs on base. Mitch Dean was summoned to the mound. Hubie Brooks ended the inning by going to the wall to snag a line drive. But our lead had been cut to 6-5.

Nyman led off the next inning by knocking the ball out of the park. We went on to score three more that inning, and we were home free. The 10-7 win advanced us to the second round against Southern Illinois.

In game two, Darrell Jackson and Jamie Allen combined for a four-hitter, and we smacked eleven hits. But we lost 3-2. We just couldn't seem to score any runs. And two of the Southern Illinois runs were caused by errors.

After the loss, I violated one of my cardinal rules of never ripping a team after a tournament loss. At practice the next morning, I assailed their intensity and hustle. A bad situation was getting worse by the minute.

About that time, Rick Peters' father, Si, who had been tremendously supportive, and who had had considerable coaching success himself in Connie Mack ball, came over and suggested politely that some guys on the team had some things they'd really like to say. I wasn't very happy. I had gone to the brink of intimidation. They weren't going to get a nice word out of me. Looking back on it, there was nothing wrong with the players. It was much more a case of me just feeling the pressure.

I isolated myself for about an hour, and just sat and prayed and thought about it. Then I called a team meeting. I was calm by then and made a short opening speech pointing out how hard we'd all worked and how far we'd come. I also reminded them of how little chance people had given us at the start of the season. I said I was sure we all knew we had the best team in Omaha and suggested we'd been getting in our own way. Or maybe I'd been getting in their way.

Then I opened up the meeting and encouraged— practically demanded—responses from all the players. They started out with some predictable comments. "Why didn't you use more pinch hitters last night?" one of the pinch hitters asked. But then remarks moved to the gut level. It ended up being a time of good, open communication. An hour after we dismissed, I heard from the players' girl friends and parents that the players thought it was the best meeting ever and that Minnesota's chances were now zero. It wasn't so much what was said as that everybody had a chance to say it.

Vasquez was a little shaky in the first inning but settled down to pitch a six-hitter, and we beat Minnesota 8-4. Henderson had two doubles and two singles, Allen had a home run, Horner, Bando, and Humphry had two hits apiece, and we had our momentum back. I was used to battling back from the losers' bracket, and I was sure we could go all the way.

154

Next up was an old nemesis, South Carolina. Bobby Richardson was gone, and the Gamecocks were led by a first-year coach with the unlikely name of June Raines (no kin to April Showers). Raines made every coaches' all-name team in the trivia league, but there was nothing trivial about the job he'd done in his first season at the major college level.

For us, now was the time to gamble. Every tournament team has to start somebody who's never started, and I figured that two relief pitchers might equal one complete game. So I decided to use the Dean-Allen combination against the unbeaten Gamecocks. Dean did not have his best stuff, but he battled hard and made very few mistakes. We went to the seventh leading 5-2. Mitch still seemed able to make the big pitch, but I knew that couldn't last. The first two hitters singled, bringing up Mark Van Bever, who had hurt us badly when South Carolina eliminated us in 1975.

What was about to take place was one of the most memorable moments in Omaha in many years. I brought in Allen, the Fireballin' Fat Man from Yakima, Washington, and the scouts got out their radar guns. But it was a somewhat subdued Allen. He seemed to be feeling the pressure of the moment and pitched carefully, but not effectively, to Van Bever, who singled. The lead runner held at third. Bases loaded, nobody out.

Occasionally during the season, we'd worked on a great pickoff play we had, the Flap Play. The reason we called it the Flap Play was that the catcher signaled for it by flapping his glove. The pitcher would see the flap of the glove, and he'd whirl and fire to the shortstop, who had snuck behind the runner at second base. The reason we called it great was that it always worked—in practice. Somehow, it had never worked in a game, probably because Bando, being a new catcher, hadn't had time to go to pickoff school yet. It involved three people, really—the pitcher, shortstop, and catcher. The timing had to be precise. If one man missed, it wouldn't work.

So with the bases loaded, Henderson decided the Flap Play was our only hope. He called time and walked all the way to the mound, which normally would have given everything away. But as he got there, he screamed at Humphry to watch out for the squeeze play while brushing his hand across his chest, the Flap signal.

Bando, a communications major, got the message. Henderson returned to his position at shortstop. Allen went to the top of the mound and looked at the catcher.

Henderson broke to second. Bando flapped his glove. Allen spun and fired to Henderson, and Mike applied the tag to the baserunner scrambling back toward the bag. He was out.

It was a big out, but the effect on Allen was even bigger. Jamie did one of the great Jekyll-Hyde acts of all time, turning from a scared freshman into a romping, stomping mixture of Mark (The Bird) Fidrych and Al (The Mad Hungarian) Hrabosky. He jumped up and down on the mound, talking to him-

156

self a mile a minute and yelling at the batters. His fastball became a blur. He struck out the next two Gamecock hitters and leaped high into the air waving his arms after each whiff. He squatted on the mound to protest calls and captivated the crowd with his antics. When the inning ended, somebody in the held out his jacket by the corners like a matador's cape, and Jamie charged it like a mad bull. The Omaha fans gave him a standing ovation.

In the three innings he worked, he struck out five, and we won 6-2, advancing to the semifinals.

Game five, the next night, was a rematch against Southern Illinois. Darrell Jackson, in his final college game, followed a script with a storybook ending.

Through most of his college career, Darrell was the least likely, unluckiest, most mixed-up pitcher I'd ever seen. Pat Kuehner had found him on a recruiting trip to California. He was striking out all the prospects we were looking at, so we offered him a scholarship.

Darrell battled through two years on the jayvee club, although he did make one appearance with the varsity as a freshman. We were playing USC at their park, and Darrell, home on Easter vacation, came to see the game. When I ran out of pitchers, I called him out of the stands. We found a uniform several sizes too large—Darrell is about five-foot-nine and 140 pounds—and he went in trembling against mighty USC.

He struck out the first two batters.

As a junior, Darrell came out for fall ball on the varsity, but one day failed to show up. The next day he came around with a bandaged hand and explained that he had cut a knuckle on his pitching hand while washing dishes, and it wouldn't heal. Three weeks later we took him to a hand surgeon, who said he had to operate.

Darrell was a very emotional young man. He had had a good Christian background, and that night as I came to see him in the hospital before the game, he was crying.

"Coach, I've got to talk to you," he told me. "I've tried to pray that God would give me one more chance, but I can't. Before God will answer me, I've got to tell you the truth."

It turned out that he had actually been in a fight and had cut his hand on someone's front tooth.

I'd always liked Darrell, and I'd been concerned about him, but this cemented a bond between us. Before I became a Christian, I might have thrown him out of the program, warning the team that anyone else who fouled up like that would go, too.

Darrell had never thrown a shutout in his college career, but against the Salukis of Southern Illinois, he spun a three-hitter, and the guys backed him with a devastating eighteen-hit attack to bury SIU 10-0.

That choked me up more than any performance in the series. I wanted him to do well, and when he pitched that semi-final game, I felt good about the positive influence of my life on a young man.

Darrell's career grand finale had placed us into another match, this time with June Raines' South Carolina Gamecocks for the national championship.

After four times of being this close and not succeeding, here I was again. Both Arizona State and South Carolina had one loss in the tournament. Whoever walked off the field ahead after nine innings would be the 1977 College World Series winner.

Jerry Vasquez was pitching for us. A fellow named Jim Lewis was throwing for the Gamecocks. Both were in command.

In the third inning, Rick Peters reached second. Mike Henderson singled sharply to left. The left-fielder got the ball quickly, and Peters held at third. As Mike got to first base, he took a wide turn.

Suddenly the throw from left came in to the first baseman behind Mike. Quickly he scuttled toward second before the first baseman could tag him.

Peters, on third, saw Henderson caught in a run-down and sprinted for the plate. He crossed just before the Gamecocks caught up with Henderson and tagged him out.

We led 1-0 . . . on a mistake. We'd run bases poorly all season. Now we did it again and scored a very big run. What could happen next?

Vasquez was struggling, even though no one had scored so far. Most of the outs were fly balls to the outfield—not a comfortable situation in a national championship game.

Leading off the seventh inning, USC's Steve King hit a fly that carried too far. The score was tied 1-1.

I made up my mind that if Jerry allowed another baserunner, I would bring in Jamie Allen.

The next man up blasted another shot into right

field. It was going deep. Hubie Brooks retreated to the base of the right field wall, leaped, and got it.

Vasquez retired the next two men, and it was our turn to bat.

Chris Bando was the second man up. He'd seen nothing but breaking balls from Lewis his first two times. This time he was looking for a fastball he could pull. He finally got one and took full advantage of it. He belted it over the right field fence, and the Sun Devils led, 2-1.

Vasquez suddenly seemed as pumped up as Allen had been against South Carolina in the first game. He retired the next five men he faced, and before I knew it, there were two outs in the ninth inning. We were one out away from victory and the national championship. The suspense was killing.

Vasquez threw, the batter swung, and popped a high foul ball between third and home.

It's funny how you remember little things at big moments. I remember the unflappable Doug Gerlach. The normally unflappable Doug Gerlach, that is. Doug was down on the field, and as the ball was popped up, he screamed, "Bando, Bando, Bando!"

Bando didn't move. Doug saw it and moaned, "Oh, what have I done?"

But third baseman Brandt Humphry drifted under the ball and squeezed it! The Devils had done it! Bedlam! Pandemonium! Joy!

And peace.

I felt as though an eight million pound weight had

just been taken off my back. It had been a long six years. I looked around at the people who'd been with me so long and was really as happy for them as for myself. In fact, they tell me I went down the line and hugged each player. I honestly can't remember exactly what happened in that jumble of screaming, happy, celebrating people. During the interview on national television, I almost broke down.

Some of my friends watching on TV told me the picture did break down, but the audio worked perfectly. They heard me say, while standing at home plate, that I wanted to praise June Raines for the greatest first-year job of coaching ever. I thanked Pat Kuehner and Roger Schmuck for their great contributions. And then I told the nation, "I would never have made it without a personal relationship with Jesus Christ."

There was nothing momentary about that high. The satisfaction has never left.

The Devils flew into Sky Harbor Airport at two in the morning to a roaring welcome from more than three thousand fans. I invited the whole team over to our house for Mexican food. All of them came, and so did the people from that airport crowd. Or so it seemed. What a celebration!

Horner, Humphry, Henderson, Nyman, Allen, and Vasquez were all named to the all-tourney team. Our second baseman Bobby Horner was also named the Series Most Valuable Player after hitting .444 with two homers and nine RBIs. Chris Bando, whose

161

brother Sal had been MVP in ASU's first NCAA championship in 1965, got the recognition of his own that he deserved.

Jerry Vasquez, who entered ASU without a scholarship, but who had just been drafted in the third round by the Texas Rangers, summed up the togetherness of this team.

"I don't want to leave, coach," he said at the party. "In fact, I'll come back next year ... if you give me a scholarship."

When the cheering and laughter finally died down and everyone left, I had a chance to reflect on the triumph that had been so long coming.

I decided winning had not been the thing I enjoyed the most. The thing I enjoyed the most was not losing. And I thought about Frank Sancet, who I'd always admired. He had a great coaching career at Arizona for more than thirty years, and yet many people remember him only as the man who never won at Omaha. I'd been afraid that was going to happen to me.

Another feeling was one of great gratitude. I was very grateful to the Architect of my life, and also thankful to the architect of Arizona State baseball, good ol' Bobby Winkles.

Then I was thankful for the scores of people who wrote notes of congratulations. They came from friends all over the country; from sports colleagues, young people, reporters, and sportscasters. Commissioner Bowie Kuhn wrote; so did archrival USC coach Rod Dedeaux. Bump sent a note, as well as

Jimmy Walker, president of the Phoenix Racquets.

Some came from people I'd never heard of. "God ministered to me through your witness for Christ," one young man wrote. Another wrote, " . . . There were many great moments and thrills . . . However, none was as great as the one I experienced after the game victory speech when you witnessed to your personal relationship with Jesus Christ."

The letter I remember the most that summer came from the head of that old posse down the road that's still chasin' Butch. One day shortly after I became a Christian, Jerry Kindall and the Wildcats were on their team bus heading to Tempe for a series with us.

Like most coaches, I suppose, Jerry was in a highly competitive state of mind when a player spoke to him.

"Coach, I heard something, but I'm not sure if it's true. I heard Coach Brock has become a Christian."

Jerry blurted out, "He can't do that!" Then he quickly realized how ridiculous that must have sounded and added, "I certainly hope it's true."

When he got to Tempe, he came to my office and chatted for a few minutes. "I heard something . . ." he hinted, " . . . and I wondered if . . ."

"If you mean that I've become a Christian, it's true," I said as I smiled at the man who was one of my toughest rivals, but now was also a brother in Christ.

Jerry wrote just a few days after we won in Omaha.

Dear Jim,

I am genuinely pleased for you and the outstanding Sun Devil team at winning the NCAA College World Series. Your perseverance and dedication to that goal was admired by every coach who knows the difficulty in reaching it. I particularly am pleased that a Christian coach has guided his team to that championship, because your testimony and witnessing can be effectively used in the future as in the past.

The Wildcats offered very little competition in '77, Jim, but watch out for Arizona in '78. Have an enjoyable summer, and may I offer one suggestion: sit back, relax, simply enjoy the championship, and forget about recruiting.

Your friend,
Jerry

JIM BROCK'S ARIZONA STATE PLAYERS WHO HAVE PLAYED IN THE MAJOR LEAGUES

Craig Swan, pitcher	New York Mets
Jim Crawford, pitcher	Detroit Tigers
Alan Bannister, shortstop	Philadelphia Phillies, Chicago White Sox
Eddie Bane, pitcher	Minnesota Twins
Jim Otten, pitcher	Chicago White Sox
Bump Wills, second base	Texas Rangers
Jim Umbarger, pitcher	Texas Rangers, Oakland A's
John Poloni, pitcher	Texas Rangers
Floyd Bannister, pitcher	Houston Astros
Ken Landreaux, outfield	California Angels

COLLEGE PLAYERS OF THE YEAR
Jerry Maddox, 1975 Lefty Gomez Plate Award
Floyd Bannister, 1976 Lefty Gomez Plate Award and
   The Sporting News Player of the Year

THE JIM BROCK RECORD

	Won	Lost	Tied	Pct.	
1966 Mesa	17	16		.515	
1967 Mesa	19	13	3	.586	
1968 Mesa	21	13		.618	
1969 Mesa	30	12	1	.709	National runner-up Regional champion State champion
1970 Mesa	39	11	1	.775	National champion Regional champion State champion
1971 Mesa	37	15	2	.704	National champion Regional champion State champion
1972 ASU	64	6		.914	National runner-up Regional champion Conference champion Division champion
1973 ASU	59	8		.881	National runner-up Regional champion Conference champion Division champion
1974 ASU	39	24		.619	
1975 ASU	61	13		.824	National third place Regional champion Conference champion Division champion

1976 ASU	65	10		.867	National third place
					Regional champion
					Conference champion
					Division champion
1977 ASU	57	12		.826	National champion
					Regional champion
					Conference champion
					Division champion

ARIZONA STATE'S RECENT ALL-AMERICANS

1972
Eddie Bane, pitcher
Alan Bannister, shortstop
Craig Swan, pitcher

1973
Eddie Bane, pitcher
Bill Berger, second base

1975
Floyd Bannister, pitcher
Jerry Maddox, shortstop
John Poloni, pitcher

1976
Floyd Bannister, pitcher
Mike Colbern, catcher
Ken Landreaux, outfield

1977
Bob Horner, second base
Hubie Brooks, outfield
Dave Hudgens, first base
Rick Peters, outfield